# Pa...
# ...as a
# hobby

### by Dennis Parker

## SAVE-OUR-PLANET SERIES

## CONTENTS

**Photographers:** Dr. Herbert R. Axelrod, David Alderton, Joan Balzarini, Michael DeFreitas, David Dube, Isabelle Francais, Michael Gilroy, Fred Harris, Pam Hutchinson, Terri Leinneweber, Irene & Michael Morcombe, Horst Mueller, Robert Pearcy, Ginny Tata-Phillips, J. Quinn, L. Robinson, San Diego Zoo, R. Sweeney, Karen Taylor, Carol Thiem, T. Tilford, Vogelpark Walsrode,

*Red-fronted Conure, Aratinga wagleri. Good health is a very important factor when purchasing a pet parrot. A healthy bird will have clear, bright eyes, and good, tight feathering.*

Distributed in the UNITED STATES to the Pet Trade by T.F.H. Publications, Inc., One T.F.H. Plaza, Neptune City, NJ 07753; distributed in the UNITED STATES to the Bookstore and Library Trade by National Book Network, Inc. 4720 Boston Way, Lanham MD 20706; in CANADA to the Pet Trade by H & L Pet Supplies Inc., 27 Kingston Crescent, Kitchener, Ontario N2B 2T6; Rolf C. Hagen Ltd., 3225 Sartelon Street, Montreal 382 Quebec; in CANADA to the Book Trade by Macmillan of Canada (A Division of Canada Publishing Corporation), 164 Commander Boulevard, Agincourt, Ontario M1S 3C7; in the United Kingdom by T.F.H. Publications, PO Box 15, Waterlooville PO7 6BQ; in AUSTRALIA AND THE SOUTH PACIFIC by T.F.H. (Australia), Pty. Ltd., Box 149, Brookvale 2100 N.S.W., Australia; in NEW ZEALAND by Brooklands Aquarium Ltd. 5 McGiven Drive, New Plymouth, RD1 New Zealand; in Japan by T.F.H. Publications, Japan—Jiro Tsuda, 10-12-3 Ohjidai, Sakura, Chiba 285, Japan; in SOUTH AFRICA by Multipet Pty. Ltd., P.O. Box 35347, Northway, 4065, South Africa. Published by T.F.H. Publications, Inc.

Manufactured in the United States of America by T.F.H. Publications, Inc.

# Introduction

There are over nine thousand species of birds and of these, without any doubt, the group known as the parrots is especially interesting for the potential pet owner. There are approximately 330 parrot species found largely in the warmer climates of the world. In size, they range from the tiny pygmy parrots of New Guinea, 3.5 in (9 cm), to the giant of the parrot world, the Hyacinth Macaw. This bird may exceed 39 in (100 cm) in total length.

The predominant color found in parrots is green, but this is often combined with other colors, such as blue, yellow, or red, to create stunningly beautiful birds. Some species carry no green and may be all white, black, gray, pink, yellow, or combinations of these. The high popularity of certain species, such as the budgerigar, lovebird, cockatiel, and others, has resulted in the appearance of many color mutations over the years. This has greatly increased the potential colors and patterns seen in these particular species.

**DOMESTIC HISTORY**

Parrots have been kept as pets for a few thousand years by the native

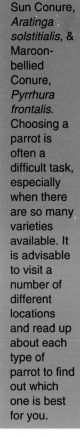

Sun Conure, *Aratinga solstitialis*, & Maroon-bellied Conure, *Pyrrhura frontalis*. Choosing a parrot is often a difficult task, especially when there are so many varieties available. It is advisable to visit a number of different locations and read up about each type of parrot to find out which one is best for you.

populace of all countries in which they are indigenous. They did not reach the western world until early explorers, such as Alexander the Great of Macedonia (356-323 BC), brought examples back to Europe. The ability of parrots to mimic sounds, including those of the human voice, ensured that these birds would forever remain a popular attraction to humans. The Romans captured thousands of various parrot species during their African conquests, and certain species, such as the Grey Parrot, became immensely popular. Texts were written on how these birds should be trained.

With the exploration of South America by the Spanish, a whole new range of highly exotic parrots was to arrive in Europe to continue the fashionable, and costly, practice of keeping birds in the homes of the wealthy. The later establishment of the British Empire completed the introduction of the world's parrot species to Europe. This saw the arrival of the gorgeous Australasian birds which were to become, and remain to this day, the most widely kept of all parrots.

It was in fact an Australian species, the budgerigar, *Melopsittacus undulatus*, that really opened the door to the keeping of parrots by the working population of western countries. During the early part of the 20th century this little parakeet was exported from its homeland by the hundreds of thousands. It proved to take readily to the colder climates of Europe, and in the USA it proved to be a reliable breeding bird. The appearance of color mutations in the

Plum-headed Parakeet, *Psittacula cyano-cephala*, is a bird that is rarely seen in captivity, but is a beautiful sight to behold.

species merely added to the already established craze of parrot keeping.

In the wake of the budgerigar came the cockatiel, along with most other Australian species from large cockatoos to little finches. So large were the numbers of birds exported from Australia that their government, in 1959, placed a ban on the export of all flora and fauna from that island continent—the ban remains to this day. The effect was a rapid development in the breeding of Australian species, and this has proved extremely successful. Most are now well established in captivity to a greater or lesser degree.

The denial of Australian species to aviculturists created an upsurge of interest in the South American parrots, as well as those of Africa and Asia. Again, this resulted in vast numbers being taken from their natural habitats to the degree that other islands and countries began to ban the export of their precious wildlife. This resulted in greater efforts to establish breeding stocks. It also stabilized the value of the birds in relation to

the cost of producing them. This was never the case when they were taken freely from the wild. Invariably, wild caught birds were much cheaper to buy than captive bred examples, so there was little encouragement to breed them. Today, there are many captive bred species available to the potential parrot owner, and the purchase of a wild caught example must be the last desirable option. Further, birds bred in captivity are by far the sounder investment, and

The Red Lory, *Eos bornea*, is a nectar feeding bird and therefore requires a special diet unlike most other parrot-like birds.

more likely to live to the full potential of their life span.

**MISCONCEPTIONS**

The tremendous popularity of the Australian parrot species early in this century created many problems for parrots that were native to other continents. The Australian species live in arid lands where vegetation is at best seasonal, and at worst almost non-existent. In order to survive, Australian parrots evolved to live on Spartan diets in comparison to the birds of tropical Africa, Asia, or South America. The fact that budgerigars and cockatiels could seemingly do well on an almost all seed diet resulted in many parrots from other regions also being fed on such a regimen.

This resulted in the

misconception that such diets were adequate for all parrots, which could not be further from the truth. Indeed, even Australian species need some fruits and greenfoods if they are to reach peak health and condition. A varied diet is absolutely essential for all parrots coming from tropical countries where fruits are found in abundance along with seeds, thus part of the natural diet for these species.

Another misconception with parrots is that they are all capable of becoming good talking birds. In fact, only a handful can be regarded as having excellent talking potential. Even among these it does not follow that all individuals will prove to be good talkers. Much depends on the age of the bird when acquired, its

Your pet shop carries a variety of foods that are an easy and fun way to feed your birds and still provide wholesome nutrition. Photo courtesy of Pretty Bird.

temperament, and the patience and skill of the owner. The general advice to the potential parrot owner must be never to purchase one of these birds in the hopes that it will become a good talker—you might be sadly disillusioned.

## PARROT VIRTUES

For most owners, the greatest single virtue of a parrot is its intelligence. With this attribute they have few equals in the avian world. Parrots can become exceedingly attached to their owner, often displaying a degree of affection that compares with that of the other leading pets—dogs and cats. They can be very amusing and will delight you with their antics. Parrots are also very long-lived animals. The very small species could easily reach ten years of age, while the cockatiel may exceed twenty years. The amazons, Grey Parrots, cockatoos, and macaws can be expected to live in excess of fifty years if cared for correctly from a young age.

In the following chapters many aspects of parrot management are discussed in order to provide you with a basic reference work on this group of birds. The

final chapter describes most of the commonly kept species so you can decide which appeal to you, and if it is suited to your particular situation.

## PARROT DESCRIPTIONS

When reading through magazines and other avicultural literature (including this book) you will see a number of descriptive terms used. These include parakeets, conures, lovebirds, lorikeets, lories, broadtails, parrotlets, cockatoos, and macaws.

An adult Senegal Parrot, *Poicephalus senegalus*, may be shy at first, but usually settles in well and tames rather quickly.

Eclectus Parrots, *Eclectus roratus*, that are kept in a large aviary are usually willing to breed. The female Eclectus (red) becomes very shy during nesting and should not be disturbed.

All of these are terms used for various parrot groups. For example, many longtailed parrots are called parakeets, while short tailed members of the order are called parrots. A broadtail is simply a common name applied to certain Australian parakeets. A macaw is longtailed, but you would not call it a parakeet, it is simply a macaw. In the USA the omnipresent budgerigar is more commonly known as a parakeet. While it is a parakeet, the term could actually refer to any one of a considerable number of parrots. This term is rather inappropriately used. As you learn more about this group of birds you will come to know to which parrots each of the special terms refers to.

# Accommodation

The accommodation you will need for your new parrot will either be an indoor cage or an outside aviary, depending on whether you plan to keep your parrot purely as a house pet, or as a breeding or aviary bird. The house pet can be accommodated either in a large cage or an indoor flight. There is no shortage of commercial cages for parrots, so you will have an extensive range to choose from, both in their design and their cost. Likewise, aviaries can be simple or very complex structures depending on how well filled your wallet is, and what your long term parrot keeping objectives are. This chapter will highlight the major considerations you should be aware of to choose the proper accommodation.

## THE PARROT CAGE

The essentials of any parrot cage are that it be large enough to comfortably house the size of the bird you are planning to purchase, be made of materials that reflect the power of your parrot's beak, and be easy to maintain in a clean condition. Of equal importance is the fact that

it should be of a design that provides the maximum of usable space, rather than being an ornate structure that actually offers a limited area for the parrot to move around in.

### Size

The cage should be large enough so that the parrot, when standing in a central position, can extend its

Green-winged Macaw, *Ara chloroptera*. Macaws pair bond for life. In keeping macaws, if space allows, it is often a good idea to begin a breeding program to propagate the species.

wings fully without touching the bars in any direction. It should also be large enough that when sitting on the highest perch, its head is at least two or more inches below the overhead bars. The tip of its tail should be at least four inches above the cage floor. These are absolute minimums! Anything less is far too small for your bird. The minimum size is only acceptable if your parrot is given ample exercise time outside of its cage. The more time it is expected to spend in the cage, the larger this should be. If your pet cannot spend at least a few hours each day outside of its cage, I would suggest that you really do

not have the time for one of these birds, and might be better considering an alternative pet. This applies to all birds, from the smallest parrots, such as budgerigars and lovebirds, to the largest of macaws. The smaller parrots could be kept in an indoor aviary and in the company of their own kind would not have the need to spend extensive hours outside of their accommodation.

**Cage Design**
   Easily, the best shape bird cage is a large rectangle. This allows maximum use of available space. Tall, round parrot cages have been popular for a few centuries, but are

not actually the best option from the bird's viewpoint. The door should be as large as possible so the bird can exit easily. This will also enable you to reach in to clean the cage without any problems. Some designs have both a large door, and the facility for one entire side to fold down to form a platform. These are well recommended.

In some designs the actual cage can be lifted totally from the base, which makes cleaning very easy. In others, there will be a pull out drawer. Some will have a weld wire floor above the drawer, others may not. Plastic is used quite a lot these days for the floor sections. This is fine providing it is not accessible to your pet's beak. Even a modest-size parrot, such as a lovebird, might easily break pieces from this. If enough of these are swallowed it could create a serious internal blockage.

The more costly cage may feature a guard around the outside of it so that any seed, other food items, or feathers that might fall to the floor or carpet of your home, will be channeled back into the cage base. This saves you a lot of cleaning. These guards can be purchased separately from a local pet store if you cannot afford or find a model with it included initially.

Pay particular attention to the way the cage door is

An outdoor aviary can add to the beauty of your yard, especially if a number of colorful parrots are added to it. The wire mesh of the aviary should be of a heavy gauge if parrots are intended to be housed.

fastened. Parrots can be regular "Houdinis" if the fastening is of a simple latch type. The main design point of the door lock should be such that it cannot be accessed by the parrot.

### Cage Materials

All parrot cages will be made of weld wire of varying thickness (gauge). The more costly models will be chromium plated, others will be galvanized to varying levels of quality. Some may be epoxy resin coated; these are suitable for the smaller parrot species. Check that there are no dangerous sharp edges protruding into the cage which could harm your pet. Also, check that the welding joints are well connected and not likely to be a trap for dirt. A cage suitable for a large parrot would of course need to be very robust, and it is likely to be a very expensive item.

### Cage Furnishings

The most important furnishings of a cage are the perches and the feed/water containers. Perches must be suited to the species you keep. Ideally, there should be two or more of differing diameters so your parrot can have adequate exercise for its feet. Commercial perches will be of smooth doweling, but they could be replaced with a suitable length of a fruit tree branch (except cherry), of willow, oak, or other available non-toxic

Green - winged Macaw, *Ara chloroptera*. Macaws require perches that are quite thick in diameter. Wooden dowels can be purchased, or natural branches from non-toxic trees can also be used.

trees. Plastic perches are not advised because the parrots will easily gnaw through them and if enough plastic is ingested, could prove harmful to the bird.

Toys are designed to prevent your bird from becoming bored and to keep it amused during the time that it must spend inside of its cage alone. Too many toys inside a bird's cage, however, may create an over crowded environment. Suggested toys are wooden ladders, rope suspended from the roof bars, wooden bobbins, twigs, and other wooden items. Avoid plastic toys, unless made specifically for certain species. Birds may splinter the toy and swallow pieces with serious consequences. The best floor covering for a cage is paper. You can place a few sheets down and remove one or two of these as they become soiled.

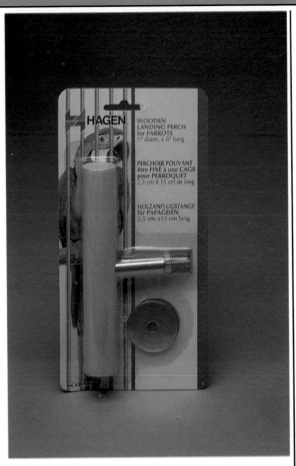

Pet shops carry an assortment of products designed to keep your bird happy. A wooden landing perch like this one is just one of the many available products that will make your bird's free time comfortable.. Photo courtesy of Rolf C. Hagen Corp.

**Play frames**

You are advised to purchase or construct a play frame for your parrot so that it can enjoy some time away from its cage. It need only be a simple framework of wooden bars and ladders that the parrot can climb up, down, and between. It should be situated on a large base so that food and water pots can be included in the design. When free flying in your room this will be the parrot's favorite place to come to.

## Parrot Stands

If you purchase a cockatoo, macaw, or other large parrot, do not try to cut accommodation costs by purchasing a parrot stand for it to live on. The fact that you may see large macaws chained to these at some zoos merely indicates the zoo's lack of understanding of these birds. A stand is useful only as a resting place, never as a home for your pet. There should never be a need to use a leg-chain on a pet bird because it can be seriously injured if it becomes frightened and attempts to jump off. Many birds have broken their legs or have been found dangling from their chain from such accidents.

## AVIARIES

There are many aspects of aviary design to consider, and the best advice you can take is to visit as many breeders as possible. By doing so, you can take note of the design in relation to the species being kept, and to its ease of cleaning. Breeders will be delighted to tell you where they feel they could improve things if they started again. Once you have discussed the many features of an aviary with a number of parrot owners, you should then make detailed plans for your own. These should then be carefully priced, and adjustments made at the planning stage. This is much easier than if you go ahead too quickly and then find you are running out of cash!

## Design

The most popular design for breeding aviaries is a line of flights, each extending from an enclosed shelter. The shelter will form part of a larger room in which you have space to store and prepare foods, keep cages, and keep all of the other things you will need for day-to-day operations. A larger set-up will have flights running along either side of a central service room.

It is very useful, where a line of flights is contemplated, to include a weld wire safety and access porch at the end of the flights, and running along the entire length of the line. There should also be a safety porch attached to the entrance to the birdroom, or to the flight entrance in a single aviary. As a precaution it is wise for you to feature double weld wire to all adjacent flights. If this is not part of the design, birds, especially chicks, could have their feet mutilated by parrots in

**Opposite:** Tucuman Amazon, *Amazona tucumana*. All parrots should be permitted to spend a great deal of time away from their cage. A nice play stand made of wood can keep a bird amused for hours.

Rose-ringed Parakeet, *Psittacula krameri*. Outdoor aviaries give parrots a great deal of room in which they can fly about and exercise.

the next flight. Chicks might even be killed. Incorporating this does double up the cost of the weld wire, but it is absolutely essential for parrots, and especially so during the breeding season. If birds of prey are resident to your area it is wise to also feature weld wire on either side of the roofing panels, or a false roof above the flight roof. This will also deter cats, rats, weasels, and their like.

Be sure that there is plenty of natural daylight in the birdroom because birds do not like entering dark shelters. All windows should be protected with weld wire to keep the birds in should the glass break. Skylights are a good idea because they let in ample light without taking up valuable wall space, which regular windows do.

If space is limited, you could feature half height internal shelters for the birds, thus giving you storage space beneath the shelter flights. The first few feet of roof from the shelter should be covered so the birds can escape direct sunshine and rain, yet still enjoy the benefit of fresh air. If strong winds are a feature of your local climate, the first part of the aviary flight sides could also be protected with a suitable covering.

If the aviary is to be a display unit, rather than one for breeding, you might consider an octagonal or circular design. These are more difficult to construct, and take up a lot of space, but do have great esthetic appeal. An aviary that runs across your line of vision also makes for esthetic appeal, especially if the entire back length is made of brick or a similar solid wall material.

## THE SITE

Ideally, the aviary should be as close to your home as possible. This makes for easier management and greater security, an important consideration these days. Do not place the aviary under overhanging branches of established trees. These present many problems— dripping rain water long after is has stopped raining, the risk of wild bird droppings falling into the flight, and the nuisance of insects during hot weather. However, the flight may need some protection from inclement weather. A wind break of poplar, willow, or spruce is a good idea. They will provide an nice backdrop to the aviary and could even be placed in large tubs so they can be moved about while they are young.

Never place the aviary at a low point of your garden. It might be at risk to flooding during heavy rainstorms. If there is no alternative, build up a solid foundation to keep the flight free from flooding. Finally, in your plans, make allowance for future expansion, and for separate quarantine and hospital housing so these are not part of your main stock building.

## MATERIALS

The materials used in erecting parrot aviaries will clearly reflect the species being kept. The smaller parakeets will not need as heavy a gauge wire as the

Outdoor aviaries can be designed in such a way that they become esthetically pleasing to have on one's property.

Blue-fronted Amazon, *Amazona aestiva*. Parrots require a great deal of exercise, either inside their cage (if it is large enough) or out. Climbing stands allow your pet freedom, and a great deal of pleasure.

be ½ x ½ in (1.25 x 1.25 cm) but this can work out to be expensive. Slightly less costly will be 1 x ½ in (2.5 x 1.25 cm) and this will keep out all but baby mice. The weld wire should be stapled onto a wooden framework of individual panels. In this way you can add to, replace, or disassemble and move entire aviaries. The frame for the panels should be of 2 x 1 in (5 x 2.5 cm) timber which has been treated with a suitable wood preservative.

For most parrots you will need to nail strips of tin or aluminum over any woodwork that is exposed to the beak of these birds, otherwise they will soon reduce it to nothing. The made up panels can be fitted onto a small brick wall, or directly onto a concrete base. An alternative to wood for the larger parrots is alloy poles. These will require more thought into the design; they will literally last a lifetime, and are safe against the most powerful cockatoo beak.

The aviary flight base should be made of concrete, or at least thick paving slabs. Bare earth floors are not only a health hazard, but are easy for mice, rats, foxes, and other potential predators to

largest cockatoos and macaws. You could use a heavy gauge, chain-link fencing for the big parrots, and then place another covering of weld wire over this to reduce the risk of predators entering the flight. This is very important because rats, weasels, and snakes can take a heavy toll on eggs and chicks.

With the risk of predators in mind, the hole size of the netting is important. The ideal would burrow into. Placing narrow holed weld wire about 12 in (30 cm) into the earth around the flight will help deter these animals. The floor of the flight should have a shallow slope to it so that rain water is taken away from the shelter end. It will also take the hosed water away when you clean the flight. Be sure to cover the exit holes that take water from the flight with fine mesh so mice cannot enter via these. You might improve the appearance of a concrete floor either by painting it with one of the outdoor pool paints, or with a covering of colored gravel. The birds will root among the gravel for grit and minerals.

The shelter for the large parrots is ideally made using brick or cinder block which will stand up better than wood to the power of their beaks. For the small to medium species a wooden shelter which is lined with a suitable insulation board will be the normal choice. Be sure that the entrance hole from the shelter to the flight incorporates a landing platform, and has a door that can be opened and closed from outside of the flight, or

from the birdroom proper. During the breeding season many parrots will not tolerate intrusions into their domain, even by their owners. This is very much so the case where the larger birds are concerned. With this fact in mind, design the aviary so that nest boxes and feeder/

The Golden Conure, *Aratinga guarouba*, also called the Queen of Bavaria Conure, is one of the most rarely seen birds in captivity.

This Blue-streaked Lory, *Eos reticulata*, is sampling a nectar mix that contains fruit.

water pots can be inspected and serviced without a need to enter the shelter or flight.

**AVIARY FURNISHINGS**

Perches are of course essential furnishings of the flight. Place these at either end so that your birds have maximum uninterrupted flying space. Natural tree branches are better than doweling. The birdroom is certainly a good place for having services hooked up to it. Water, electricity, and sewage disposal will make attending to day-to-day chores much easier. Background heating may be required for some species during the winter, but never have the birdroom so hot that it

actually increases the risk of chilling the birds when they leave it to sit in the flight. Parrots, once acclimatized, are very hardy birds.

An ionizer is a useful appliance in the birdroom as it greatly reduces the risk of bacterial build up and the dust level. This appliance comes in a range of sizes and is economic to operate. Fresh air vents are also strongly suggested, both high in the birdroom and low down (covered with fine mesh). Ventilation is crucial where many birds are housed. It is a basic part of sound husbandry techniques that will minimize the occurrence and spread of disease.

You might feature a large rooting box in the aviary flight. Plantings cannot survive any but a few selected species of parrot, so by placing clumps of grass (complete with roots), as well as wild plants, your birds can forage in these until they are all eaten. You can then clean and replenish the boxes. These boxes will be a sure hit with your bird, regardless of its species, but are especially beneficial to the ground feeding parrots.

All aviary and birdroom entrances should be fitted with strong locks. Unfortunately, parrot thefts are becoming more common. An exterior night light over the birdroom door would be a prudent investment for the little it costs.

## AVIARY SIZE

The length, width, and height of the aviary flight will no doubt reflect the space and cash you have available. As minimums, you should think in terms of 10 x 3 x 6 ft (3 x 0.9 x 1.8 m). Esthetically, 7 ft (2.1 m) is superior for the height. Flight length is always more important than width, so make this as long as possible. The size of the parrot is not necessarily indicative of the required length, though obviously the giant species should have as much space as possible, at least 20 ft (6 m) of flight length. The strong flying Australian parakeets cover large distances between feeding grounds, so these should be given long flights to exercise their wings. Amazons and Grey Parrots spend more time climbing among branches. While they are larger than many parakeets, they do not necessarily need such long flights—increased flight width might be better for them, and more branches can be featured.

These 5 week old Jandaya Conures, *Aratinga jandaya*, will soon be ready to leave the nest. They are almost fully feathered, and are not too far off from being weaned.

# Feeding Parrots

When feeding any parrot species, observe that the diet is always varied and fresh. You should find out as much as possible about the general terrain that is native to your parrot as if it were a wild bird. This will tell you quite a lot about the things it would normally eat. For example, a parrot living in a lush jungle that received a goodly amount of rain would probably include quite a lot of fruits and other green foods in its diet. Conversely, the parrots of the Australian hinterland subsist on diets that are largely made up of seeds. The situation is not the same on the Australian coast, where the vegetation can be lush, and fruits plentiful.

Parrot owners can rarely duplicate the foods that the birds would eat in the wild, but most species will accept alternatives of a similar type. The important thing is that their diet represent a reasonable reflection of the food range they are known to eat in their wild habitat. It must also reflect the size of the bird.

## GENERAL FEEDING COMMENTS

Parrots are as variable in their attitude to foods as

**Facing page:** Lesser Sulphur-crested Cockatoo, *Cacatua sulphurea*. Parrots require a well balanced diet that offers a lot of variety. Like humans, birds become bored if they are fed the same thing day after day.

Grey Parrot, *Psittacus erithacus*. Parrots have an amazing ability to use their feet as we would our hands. It is not difficult for a parrot to stand on a perch with one foot, and hold a piece of food with the other.

Although the beak of the Scarlet Macaw, *Ara macao*, is very large and powerful, it seems to use the utmost of caution when taking food from one's hand.

are dogs, cats, and humans. Some could be said to be text book feeders, meaning they accept all the foods that are generally considered typical for their species. Others are far more selective, and will refuse items that books say they should eat with relish. Taste is an acquired sense. Many birds may initially refuse a food that they will later come to enjoy. Very often an owner is heard saying "My parrot will not eat this or that food—I tried it once and it showed no interest at all," and matters are left at that. Bear in mind that animals, of which we are one species, become familiar with given items from a very

young age. When presented with the unfamiliar we may choose to ignore it, or nibble at it and then toss it aside. Slowly, if that item is offered to us again and again, we may suddenly find that we have "acquired a taste" for the food. Sometimes it may only be because we were very hungry and it was the only item on offer. Your parrot is subject to these remarks.

Some birds may have never received a wide ranging diet, or its breeder may have given it only certain items. Birds are also subject to variation in their diet during the breeding season that they might otherwise largely ignore. Live foods, such as insects, are possibly the best example of this aspect. For many years it was generally held that parrots should not eat meat, but to apply generalizations to every parrot species can be misleading; it results in misconceptions.

Quite a number of parrots enjoy a small amount of cooked meat on a non-splintering bone, such as beef or lamb. Most parrots enjoy fruits of various kinds, but some fruits are enjoyed more than others. The only way you will ever know which are favored by your particular birds is if you offer a wide range over a long enough period to establish this, and if you carefully observe your birds.

Parrots are rather wasteful feeders, so it is prudent to supply all fresh foods in small pieces. They will tend to nibble on each item and then cast it aside. Like humans, they make little distinction between what is good for them and what is not. This means you must monitor what they eat. When given free access to soaked millet seed on the ear, many will happily subsist almost entirely on this. Therefore supplies must be regulated. In this manner the birds are forced to eat other items offered, and you are able to ensure they are receiving a balanced diet. To this, access to fresh water 24 hours a day must be available.

Seed, in its various forms, should always be available to your parrots. Fresh foods, meaning plant matter, vegetables, fruits, and other items, are best given early in the morning, or in the late afternoon. This way they do not sour so easily as a result of the peak day sunlight, thus heat. Uneaten fresh foods should be removed and discarded each day. You will soon get to know, by trial and error, how much fresh food your birds will

Blue-fronted Amazon, *Amazona aestiva*. Parrots require a balanced seed mixture, as well as fresh fruits and vegetables, as a regular diet.

consume at any given sitting. If they gobble it all up, they are not getting enough—if a lot is left over, they are getting too much. Be sure to place fresh foods in a shaded part of the cage or aviary to help preserve their freshness for as long as possible.

The diet should reflect the activity level and environment of your parrot. An aviary bird will require more protein foods, especially in the colder months, than a bird living in a centrally heated home. It will also eat more energy foods because it will no doubt be more active. If your bird starts to become overweight do not starve it, but simply reduce the protein seed content until the desired weight is attained. This can take quite some time, so do not expect rapid weight loss like we try to achieve.

Vitamin and mineral supplements are important to include in your bird's diet. Products such as this come in a variety of sizes and can be purchased at your local pet store. Photo courtesy of Hagen.

## FOOD CONTAINERS

You will find that your pet shop has a range of feeding containers suited to the species you are keeping. These will either be of the open type, or of the automatic dispensing type. The automatic dispensers are usually favored by owners of small parrots, with crock or metal open dishes being used by those with larger species. Always be sure that the opening that feeds the trays of automatic dispensers is wide enough to release the larger seeds without clogging the hole. A gentle tap several times a day will ensure the seeds fall as they should. If open dishes are used, be sure to blow the husks away on a daily basis otherwise it can look as though there are plenty of seeds in the dish when there are none! If a bird is known to be a

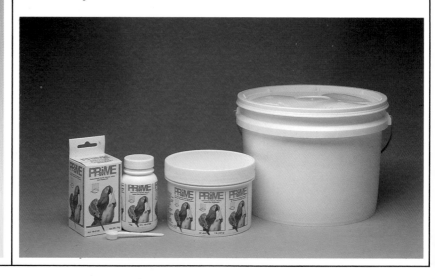

ground feeder in the wild, sprinkle some seeds on the cage or aviary floor so it can feed in a way that is natural to it. You could simply place feeding trays on the concrete or slab floor of the shelter part of the aviary where cleaning is made easier.

Fruits and vegetables can be placed into crock dishes, while cuttlefish bone and greens can be clipped to the sides of the cage or aviary. Water is best supplied to the smaller parrots via a dispenser, with an open dish being used for the large species.

Grit is essential to all birds because they have no teeth and need this to help crush the seeds and other foods in their stomach. Supply grit in its own container. The grit size should be suited to the species of parrot you keep—it is sold at pet stores and ensures that the birds receive the needed mineral intake. Crushed egg or oyster shell are other ways of supplying grit, but do ensure it is always available to your birds.

**POPULAR SEEDS**

The range of seeds available today is greater than at any other time. They range in size from very small, such as millet, canary seed, maw, rape, and the like, through the

Goffin's Cockatoo, *Cacatua goffini.* Traveling with your bird on short trips is made easier by placing the bird inside a carrying case. There are different sizes available for different sized birds, and most come equipped with seed and water dishes for easier feeding.

Vitamin and mineral fortified stove top mixes are available from your local pet shop. These easy to prepare mixes can even be frozen for quick microwave preparation. Photo courtesy of Pretty Bird.

larger seeds such as sunflower, peanuts, and mung beans, and many larger nuts. You will feed medium to small parrots with the smaller seeds up to the size of sunflower, while offering them the larger nuts in a crushed or maybe soaked form. The big parrots can be given virtually any seeds and nuts. They may take some time to eat any quantity of the smaller seeds, but this will provide them with good therapy, and they do enjoy many of the small seed varieties.

You can purchase seeds either loose or packaged. The packaged seeds are usually of a mixed type prepared for the owner of one or two birds. Breeders

find it far more convenient and cost effective to purchase individual seed varieties by the pound. This way they are able to make up their own preferred mixes to suit the needs of the time of the year. During the winter, birds will need extra protein and fat seeds, as they will during the breeding period. The rest of the year they need more energy seeds and less fattening foods.

Seeds that are rich in carbohydrates (energy) include canary, any of the millets (that on the ear in the form of sprays is relished by all parrots), maize, wheat, and sweetcorn (corn on the cob is especially liked). Protein rich seeds are pine nuts, peanuts (unsalted), rape, linseed, sunflower (striped is the most liked, black the least), hemp, niger, and maw. Sunflower, peanuts and pine nuts are also the richest in terms of their fat content. Soybean, mung beans, the seeds of grasses, and many seeds of flowers, are all examples of other seeds that can be tried.

Very often, if a seed is refused in the dry state it will be more readily taken when soaked or sprouted. To soak seed, place a small quantity of the seed in a shallow dish of water and leave it to soak for 24 hours. Rinse it under tap water to remove toxins before feeding it to your parrots. The vitamin and general food value of the seed rises, apart from which it is softer and more easily digested.

Soaked seeds are beneficial to breeding birds, their young, and birds recovering from an illness. Soaking the seed and then leaving it in a warm darkened cupboard for another 24-36 hours should prompt small shoots to appear. Seed in this state is very much a relished treat for your birds. Always rinse the seeds before feeding (which applies to all green foods and fruits). Discard any uneaten portions after a few hours.

Always purchase the finest quality seeds because these will be the most nutritious. Cheap seeds usually have been poorly stored, are not well cleaned, and have a reduced food value. Seed must always have a polished look to it, should never be cracked and rancid, and should be stored in a cool, dry place that is totally protected from the attentions of mice, rats, or wild birds.

You will find that most parrots enjoy toasted or baked wholemeal bread. They seem to drop most of it but enjoy its texture. You can place a little butter, or

A Grey Parrot, *Psittacus erithacus*, enjoys eating a piece of broccoli. Many parrots enjoy a variety of fresh fruits and vegetables as additions to their daily diet.

meat extract, on it to heighten its taste. Hard dog biscuits are also enjoyed by the larger birds.

**PLANT FOODS**

Carrots, celery, spinach, watercress, lettuce, cauliflower stalks, beans, peas, beet tops, lentils, parsley, and their like are all vegetables that will be eaten in varying degrees of enjoyment. Some, such as carrots and spinach, have a much higher food value than others, such as lettuce. Feeding is a complexity that meets both the metabolic and psychological needs of the individual. This is very important with an intelligent animal like a parrot. In the desire to make feeding easier, and have foods that store longer in the shops, too much

A young Grey Parrot, *Psittacus erithacus*, should be given an assortment of foods. This will help the bird become accustomed to eating a variety at a young age.

emphasis is placed on "complete" diets. These are fine because they are balanced, but should never totally replace the fresh foods that satisfy the psychological needs of animals to make selections from those foods they enjoy, and those which are not consumed in a matter of minutes.

Fruits that will be relished include apples, grapes, cherries, dates, figs, oranges, peaches, and bananas. Some parrots will display an obvious preference for a certain type of apple, so always bear this in mind when feeding these. Other fruits may also be consumed according to individual bird preferences. Fruits in their dried form will of course have a substantially increased constituent content—carbohydrates, proteins, vitamins, etc.

Wild plants that you can feed include chickweed, dandelion, shepherd's-purse, coltsfoot, and grasses. Berries, such as blueberry, raspberry, and strawberry, are very much liked, as are most nuts. Nuts are easier for the larger parrots with powerful beaks to cope with, but for smaller parrots they can be crushed. Always provide your birds with small branches of fruit trees because these will not only amuse them for long

The Mitred Conure, *Aratinga mitrata*, has very little red on its head compared to that of the Red-masked Conure whose red extends to the back of its head.

Jandaya Conure chick, *Aratinga jandaya.* Conures make wonderful pets especially if acquired when young. Try to inquire from your local pet shop what might be the earliest age you could purchase a parrot.

periods, but will provide important fiber content.

**PROTEIN RICH FOODS**

Many dairy and other products, plus foods formulated for rearing other birds (canaries in particular) may be appreciated by your parrots, and especially so during the breeding season. Examples are bread soaked in low fat milk, peanut butter, cheese, meat extracts, slithers of white fish, cod liver oil, and honey. Some can be given as is (e.g. cheese), or they can be prepared in the form of moist mashes held together by water or any other liquid after they have been mixed with something like bread crumbs or regular breakfast oats. Uneaten mashes must be discarded after a few hours. You can make up any concoction, and you will find all sorts of menus in specialized books

on your chosen parrot. Be careful, however, with the use of honey, which might attract bees and wasps, and with milk, which sours rather quickly, especially in warm weather.

Never be afraid of experimenting with a food item as long as you are sure it is not poisonous and is not a silly food, such as candy or a similar very sweet and artificially flavored item. It is worthwhile studying field guides to find out if any of the plants known to form part of the diet of the species you keep are available in your country. To introduce an item you feel your birds should be eating, withhold favored items until later in the day. This will encourage your parrots to try the new food. Obviously, if your parrot has refused a given item in spite of all your ploys to get it to take it over a period of time, then clearly further persistence will be wasted effort and cost. Very often people give up on their birds too soon. Just because your parrot only takes an item in very small quantities, now and then, does not mean the item is unneeded. It is the total variety intake that makes for a truly balanced diet. This means the foods eaten everyday through those taken spasmodically.

Certain species of parrots, such as the lories and lorikeets require special diets. They require a nectar formula. This can be supplied via commercially made products, or can be a homemade concoction featuring honey, condensed milk, and other similar ingredients. If you decide to obtain any of the nectar feeding parrots (which also of course eat seed and fruits) you are advised to purchase a book on these in which their diet will be discussed in more detail.

Ornate Lory, *Trichoglossus ornatus. All lories* require extra care because of their special dietary needs.

Red-masked Conure, *Aratinga erythrogenys*.
Conures are a medium sized parrot that one can
accommodate for more easily than an amazon or a
macaw.

# Selecting a Parrot

A parrot has a long life expectancy and therefore may be living with you for very many years. Its selection should be given considerable forethought. Many owners make the major mistake of rushing the selection process only to be regretful after a purchase has been made. There are many potential pitfalls with these birds, especially when you are considering the medium to larger species. The first question you should ask yourself is if you really do have the desire and the time to devote to a parrot. These birds are extremely gregarious, and must have constant companionship, if not yours then of their own kind.

**PURCHASE YOUNG BIRDS AS PETS**

If a pet bird is the objective, you must be very sure it is a young bird otherwise you may find it difficult, if not impossible, to get it really tame. The problem here is that in many species the age of the bird cannot be determined once it has gone through its first molt, which can be as early as six months of age, depending on the species. This means that choosing the right breeder or dealer to buy from is a crucial part of your selection process. The unscrupulous seller will not hesitate trying to palm off an old bird onto you.

A young parrot will often have a dark gray iris that becomes brown or white as it matures. The scales on its legs will be smooth when compared with older birds. The coloration of an immature bird

It is clear to see that some parrots are more playful than others such as this Canary-winged Parakeet, *Brotogeris versicolorus*, lying on its back.

Blue and Gold Macaw, *Ara ararauna*, & Grey Parrot, *Psittacus erithacus*. It is becomming more common to find domestic, hand-reared baby parrots available in pet stores. They do cost more than an adult bird, but are well worth it because much time is saved in taming.

will normally be that of the female of the species, if the species is dimorphic. Dimorphic is a term which means that the cocks and hens can be differentiated based on their plumage color. Young birds invariably display duller plumage than adults. They may sometimes be identified by the lack of a certain color in the plumage.

The best option for a potential pet is a hand-reared youngster, but this is also the more expensive option. It is well worth the extra cost where the medium to larger parrots are concerned. Failing this, a straight from the nest baby that is independent

of its parents is the next best choice, followed by an immature, or under one year old bird. You may be able to accurately establish the age of an immature parrot if it is of a certain species where leg banding is the norm. In these birds the breeder places a year dated, metal band on the leg of each chick so you can be sure of its age. Species that are often banded include budgerigars, lovebirds, cockatiels, and parakeets. Today, most captive bred birds are required to be banded. The band must be of the closed metal type. There are many types of open bands, including those made of metal, but these can be fitted at any age, and are not a reliable means of determining the age of a bird.

A final comment regarding the age of parrots. Remember the comments made about the longevity of some species. If you are fifty years old and purchase a baby Grey Parrot, or similar bird, the chances are good that it will outlive you. What will become of it then? I suggest that you

relative, or sold to a stranger, which is a sad way for a long time devoted companion to end its own days.

**CHOOSE THE MOST SUITABLE SPECIES**

Very often, a pet owner will purchase a given parrot simply because he/she likes the idea of owning that particular species. The negatives associated with the bird are not always considered, and are only found out after a large amount of cash has been expended. For

ponder this aspect carefully and choose only those species (the smaller ones) that you would reasonably expect to outlive. In this way, they are not passed on to some uncaring

A Green-cheeked Amazon, *Amazona viridigenalis*, displaying the bright red forehead and lores characteristic of the species.

example, the cockatoos and macaws, in particular, have tremendously loud voices that can be heard a few blocks away if they decide to screech out. Even relatively small parrots, such as many of the conures, have raucous voices that might deeply offend your neighbors—and indeed you and other members of your household.

Wild caught parrots, those that are left on their own for long periods, or those which are neglected, are the most likely birds to screech out using their natural voice. The well cared for single pet is more likely to refrain from using its natural voice too often. Aviary

parrots will always use their voice at some time, so bear this in mind if you live in a densely populated district. If neighbors complain about the noise, and this is substantiated, your local council can insist you get rid of your bird(s). The small species, such as budgerigars, lovebirds, cockatiels, and many of the Australian parrots, are not noisy, some even have pleasant whistles. However, few of the Australian parakeets make a suitable choice as pets, but are a super choice for aviary breeding.

Another aspect of parrots is that they possess very powerful beaks, again especially the larger species. A cockatoo or macaw could reduce even the hardest of furniture timber to matchsticks without a great deal

The Salmon-crested Cockatoo, *Cacatua moluccensis*, is a very affectionate bird that enjoys having its head and neck scratched.

of effort! They could also remove or mutilate a person's finger if they were mishandled. But even a relatively small parrot, such as a lovebird, can inflict a nasty little wound to a finger if it is not totally tame. Having a large parrot where there are very young children may not be a good idea. If it should bite the child, the usual result is that it is banished to live in its cage. This is a totally unethical way of keeping a bird.

Yet another aspect related to this matter of the bird's beak is of course the fact that a large parrot's accommodation will cost substantially more than that for the very small species. Apart from its size, the cage or aviary will need to be constructed so that the parrot cannot destroy any exposed woodwork. All metal cages for medium to large parrots are rather expensive, though you can dramatically reduce the cost of these if you are a handyperson, and can make your own.

Do not assume that because one parrot species is more costly than another, it will make a

This Jandaya Conure, *Aratinga jandaya*, is exhibiting its playful personality. Many birds will only perform like this if they are well trained.

Military Macaw, *Ara militaris*. Young macaws can be identified by the dark coloration of the eyes.

better pet. There is no parrot that can surpass the cockatiel for all around excellence, yet this is probably (the budgerigar excepted) the least costly of any parrot species. Cost is related to either the degree of rarity or to availability at any given time, not to any other aspect.

Another aspect you should consider when selecting a parrot is its nutritional needs. This is not generally a problem for most species, but certain birds, such as the lorikeets, while adorable pets, do need extra consideration with their diet because they are nectar feeders. This means they can also be rather messy, because their fecal matter is very liquidy.

**THE MATTER OF HEALTH**

Regardless of any other consideration, your parrot must be healthy when you obtain it. Once again, the home bred bird is the better choice. When purchasing a parrot, especially one that is expensive, be sure that its health is guaranteed in writing before you part with cash. A veterinary examination and signed certificate should be obtained with such a bird. If this is not obtainable a few pointers are as follows:

1. Inspect the conditions the birds are living under. These should be spacious and very clean. Dirty or badly worn perches, excess fecal matter in the cage, and dirty food and water containers, are a clear indication of poor management—you do not want a bird from such a source. The birds should show nice, round, clear eyes with no discharge. There should be no swelling of the cere (the fleshy area around the top of the beak).

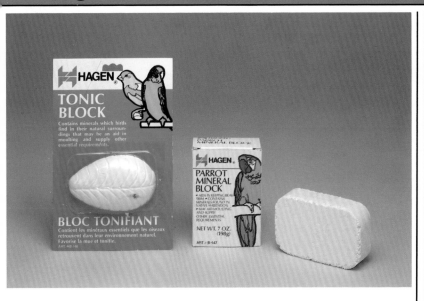

2. The feathers should be neat and clean. The odd broken feather is not a problem, it will be replaced at the first or next molt. Bald areas on the body may suggest a parasitic infection that may or may not be cured, or it could indicate a feather plucker. Missing feathers on the head are usually indicative of feather plucking by cage mates or by the parents. Birds resort to plucking out of boredom and may refrain from this once established in your home or aviary. However, it is a habit, and habits are not always cured, so avoid such a bird irrespective of what you are told by the seller.

3. Hold the bird on its back and inspect the vent area. This should be clean and not stained from liquid fecal matter, which would suggest a problem, present or recent. Feel the flesh on either side of the breastbone. This should be ample and never hollowed. A protruding breastbone indicates a nutritional deficiency known as "going light" or some other problem that has caused a rapid weight loss. This is very hard to correct.

4. Check that the claws are all present. There should be two toes that point forward, and two facing backwards. This arrangement is known as being zygodactyl. It is common to all parrot-like birds. A missing claw may not affect a pet bird, but is undesirable in breeding or exhibition stock. If the scales on the legs appear to be standing out from the leg, leg mites could be present. A crusty

appearance on and around the beak also indicates a mite problem that originates from unclean accommodations and perches. In general, the birds should move around their perches with ease, and show no problems in flapping their wings. Young parrots may be a little nervous when approached if they are not already hand tamed. They will tend to seek refuge in the corners of their cage.

5. Beware of a parrot that fluffs up its feathers and stands defiantly when you attempt to go near it, or to touch it. Its eyes will dilate and it will not hesitate to bite you if you persist in getting closer. This is no baby bird. It is not one you will tame

easily, so leave it where it is!

6. You should also take care if you see a parrot advertised as an unwanted pet in your local paper. It may be a real screecher, or have developed the bad habit of nipping if it is hand tame. It may also have proved very destructive when allowed out of its cage. These things you are unlikely to find out until after it is taken home.

**WHERE TO PURCHASE**

The only places you should even think about purchasing from are well established, reputable pet shops, breeders, and bird farms. Never purchase from open markets, and avoid buying through mail order

The Green-winged Macaw, *Ara chloroptera*, and the Hyacinth Macaw, *Anodorhynchus hyacinthinus*, have the largest beaks among birds of the parrot world.

Lesser Sulphur-crested Cockatoo,
*Cacatua sulphurea*. Cockatoos will often
fluff their feathers to appear larger than
they really are as a defense mechanism
towards something they feel threatening.

The orange colored thigh feathers of the Black-headed Caique, *Pionites melano-cephala*, make it appear as if the bird is wearing "pantaloons."

if you can. It is always better to see what you are getting at the time. There are some excellent mail specialists, but there are also some crooks. As a first time owner you should be able to locate your chosen species within your own area. Avoid places that are staffed with people who do not know about birds. Give your business to those who can give you proper service before, during, and after the sale.

By visiting one or two bird shows, ideally one devoted to parrot-like birds, you will be able to see a good range of parrots, and meet breeders and exhibitors. The show is a great source to really learn what is on offer, and to get some sound advice on the species you are most interested in. If you follow the advice in this chapter it will be repaid by your obtaining a delightful bird that will become an integral part of your future life.

# A Parrot In The Home

Having a parrot share your home with you is a major undertaking that should only be contemplated if you are prepared to commit totally to this. A parrot, especially one of the larger species, is very comparable to a child. It can easily become bored, needs lots of attention and affection, and is capable of traits such as jealousy. In this chapter, we will consider many of the obvious, and the not so obvious things you should know about living with a parrot.

## SITING THE CAGE

The cage should always be situated in the most used room, which is generally the main living area. Your parrot needs to be with you as much as possible if it is to be totally integrated in your family. The cage should not be

On very nice days you may choose to place your bird's cage outside providing there is a shaded area for it to retreat to if desired. This Lesser Sulphur-crested Cockatoo, *Cacatua sulphurea*, seems to enjoy the sunshine.

placed where it is exposed to any drafts, nor where it will receive the full intensity of sunlight. It should also be placed at a height that is both convenient for you to reach into without bending, and such that your pet is almost at eye level with you. It will feel much more secure with this than if you tower over it when you approach the cage. The cage should also sit on a very firm base so there is no chance it could be accidentally knocked over. If you have an alcove that will accommodate the cage, this will be all the better because it will give your pet a greater sense of security. This is most important with the more nervous bird. Avoid placing

Blue-fronted Amazon, *Amazona aestiva*. Chew toys are available for all sized parrots. Smaller parrots cannot chew very hard wood which should be accounted for when placing a toy in the bird's cage.

the cage over a heater unit as this will create temperature fluctuations when it switches on and off. Parrots can cope with gradual changes in the heat level, but sudden changes are likely to induce a chill.

## THE NEW ARRIVAL

Always try to collect your new parrot as early in the day as possible. This will give it plenty of time to familiarize itself with its new surroundings. Be sure to ask the seller exactly what seeds and other foods it has been receiving. The diet should remain unchanged for a few days, unless it is a case that it has lacked needed items such as fruit and green foods. You can widen the range of seeds and the rest of the diet once it has settled well into your home.

Once the bird is placed into its new cage carry on life as normal, and talk softly to your parrot as you attend your regular chores. Do not let children pester the bird because this will slow down the familiarization process. Let the bird have at least a day or two in which to observe what is going on around it. If it is a hand-reared parrot the acclimatization process is somewhat different. It

will no doubt be happy to be handled within a few hours of arrival in its new home, and you can offer it favored treats through the bars.

## WATCH WHAT YOU SAY

If you have purchased an amazon or Grey Parrot, be aware that they do pick up sounds very quickly. For example a ringing telephone, a barking dog, or a screaming baby. These particular birds can be so good at mimicry that you

Blue and Gold Macaw, *Ara ararauna*. Macaws are wonderful pets because of the genuine affection they tend to display towards their owner.

Green-cheeked Amazon, *Amazona viridigenalis*. Upon first taming a parrot, do not become alarmed if the bird holds your hand with its beak. Many times, a bird will only do this gently. If you suddenly jerk your hand while the bird is doing this, it may hold a little harder and inflict a bite.

will be running to a phone that is not ringing! If you are prone to shouting at your child, other pets, or your marital partner, beware of doing this in front of the parrot. It may just copy you—which could be embarrassing if friends are present when it chooses to repeat your words.

## HAND TAMING

There has been much written about how to hand tame a parrot. One major question is, should the wings be clipped or not, and if clipped, which is the favored method? Experts differ in their views. This author feels that as long as the method includes no rough handling, nor frightens the bird, both of which are counter productive, you should receive favored results.

I prefer to tame a bird while it is in the cage because this removes problems related to it being free to fly away, or to flutter in panic if it already has clipped wings. If it is totally happy with the close presence of your hand, which is essential in cage training, it will have no fears once it is out of the cage. Indeed, it will be more than happy to alight on your finger if it feels a little insecure when making its first trip away from its cage.

To train your parrot without letting it out of the cage, you must spend time close to the cage, preferably in the evening when your pet is already in a quiet mood. Be sure there are no distractions, such as other people present, a radio, or TV. With your hand in the cage offer the bird a favored tidbit. Once it will take this readily without moving off the perch onto the side bars, you can slowly move your finger

Red-lored Amazon, *Amazona autumnalis*. To succeed in training a parrot it is often necessary to work with the bird away from its cage, in a corner of the room, and close to the floor with a wooden dowel.

towards its chest. Repeat this many times while you talk to the parrot. Eventually, you can gently press your finger against its lower chest and it will either step onto this or retreat.

You must continue with this method until your pet will alight on your finger whenever you present this to it. Always bear in mind that birds will only step upwards, never downwards, so your finger must be placed so that this can be effected. The process may be completed within an hour or so, or it may take a few days depending on the age, personality, and background history of the bird. Never rush this initial training as it is the

platform for all that will follow. Your pet must feel very confident in you.

You may have to experience a nip when the parrot first tests your finger. This is not done out of malice, but to see how solid this new material (from the bird's viewpoint) is. This can be somewhat of a nerve racking experience for you if the bird has a powerful beak, so never risk rushing and frightening your pet because it may then nip out of fear, which is a totally different matter. If you are at all unsure of your pet, you might use a short, hand-held perch for it to stand on. Either way, once the bird will alight onto this, it can be allowed out of its cage and you will more readily be able to return it to the cage after it has had a fly around.

I do not favor wing clipping, but if circumstances dictate this is the preferred state, it is better that both wings are clipped evenly. This will allow the bird to flutter in a straight line, rather than in a half circle, which is what will happen if only one wing is clipped. The amount trimmed from the flight feathers will determine how much lift is possible. The clipped wings will be molted out each year and new feathers will replace these. By careful trimming of alternate flight feathers the parrot will not look as if it has clipped wings when in the perched position. Never cut too much away otherwise you may cause bleeding. Let your vet or an experienced parrot owner show you how to attend to this task first before doing so on your own.

The Lilac-crowned Amazon, *Amazona finschi*, is quite a talanted mimic that learns to talk very well.

## BEAK AND FEATHER CARE

If your parrot is given a sound diet, its beak should not become overgrown. Should this happen, however, it can be trimmed with a suitable pair of canine nail clippers. Again, allow your vet to show you how much to trim so as not to cause pain and bleeding. Better still, after the vet has trimmed the beak, ensure that twigs and other hard objects are available so the beak does not grow too long.

The nails can be trimmed in the same fashion if they grow overlong. This is usually the result of perches that are too small in diameter, so provide stouter perches. It is best to supply perches of differing diameters so your pet has good exercise for its feet.

When a parrot lives in a home environment, the air is usually rather dry which adversely affects the plumage. To overcome this, purchase a spray bottle and fill it with warm (never hot or cold) water. Spray the bird about 2-3 times a week. Once it is familiar with its shower it will open

This Jandaya Conure, *Aratinga jandaya*, is growing a number of new head feathers. The small white shafts enclose almost fully developed feathers.

This Blue-fronted Amazon, *Amazona aestiva*, seems to enjoy watching the fish. Fish tanks should be covered while your birds are out to avoid unnecessary accidents.

its wings and hang upside down on perches in order to maximize on the spray. Parrots really enjoy being sprayed and afterwards will carefully preen their feathers. Such care will result in super feathers that will have a beautiful appearance. During the annual molt this spraying will greatly help your bird to shed its old feathers while the new ones will grow under optimum conditions. Never neglect this aspect otherwise the feathers will become dry and brittle.

## SAFETY IN THE HOME

When your new pet is allowed out of its cage, check that the room holds no dangers for it. Open fires must be protected with a mesh screen at all times—the same being true of small bar type electric heaters. In open plan living/kitchen designs, be sure extractor fans are not on when the pet is free flying. Likewise, do not let your pet out of its cage when you are cooking.

Make sure all external doors and windows are closed, and place some

This Jandaya Conure, *Aratinga jandaya*, does not seem to like having a kitten so close by. It is best not to allow your birds to interact with cats or dog

form of net curtains over the windows. If a fully flighted parrot was to fly into a glass window or door it could easily kill itself, or at least be badly injured by the impact. Be sure aquariums are fitted with a protective cover or hood. Wiring to appliances (TV, heaters, etc.) should be neatly fitted where the bird is not likely to nibble on them.

Indoor plants are best removed from the vicinity of your pet. Some may be poisonous. Those that are not may be eaten or chewed, a state you would not wish your cherished plants to be in. Never leave

Blue-fronted Amazon, *Amazona aestiva.* Colorful toys catch a bird's attention. Once a parrot takes a liking to a particular toy, it may be difficult to take it away from it.

**Facing page:** Nanday Conure, *Nandayus nenday.* Very often parrots become amused with simple household objects such as this Nanday Conure with a toothbrush. Other favorites are broom bristles, toothpicks, and cardboard from the inside of a paper towel roll.

expensive ornaments on shelves that your parrot may alight on. They may be knocked over as it flaps its wings. Of course, if you have a larger parrot, always be present when it is free flying in the room, otherwise it may decide to give its beak a little exercise on your costly furniture or other items.

If you have a dog or cat, you must always be present when your pet bird is out of its cage, or remove the dog or cat from the area. Cats and dogs will usually ignore the larger parrots, which are well able to inflict a nasty bite if provoked. But it is still best to play safe; be present to intervene if needed.

## MIMICRY & TALKING

Most parrots have a talent to mimic sounds, including the human voice. Some, such as the Grey Parrot, many amazons, cockatoos, macaws, and budgerigars, are more talented at this than others. Never purchase your parrot purely as a potential talking bird, but rather for its character. If it does learn to talk, this is a bonus. Teaching to talk is a matter of repeating simple words on a regular basis. Only progress to sentences once the bird has spoken a few words.

Training requires great patience, and is best done when you are alone with your parrot. If your parrot is able to hear songbirds, either real ones, or records of their song, it may well copy these, which is a real treat for you. If you keep two or more pet parrots, it is far less likely that they will mimic words or sounds, but it is not unheard of, especially if one of them has already mastered numerous sounds. Generally, if you wish to own a devoted parrot, it is best to keep just one. However, if you are not able to spend long periods of time with your pet, then do acquire a companion for it. Their antics will amuse you, and they will be altogether happier than being left alone.

## THE PARROT "BUG"

What invariably happens once the parrot "bug" has bitten you is that if you have a delightful parrot, you will probably purchase another—and then another. They can grow on you just as cats and dogs can.

Citron-crested Cockatoo, *Cacatua sulphurea citrinocristata*, and Blue-fronted Amazon, *Amazona aestiva*.

Beware of jealousies in the multi-parrot home, especially if the birds are of differing sizes, or if there are two hens and a cock, or vice versa, of the same species.

If you obtain a hen parrot, one day she may present you with a clutch of eggs! She does not need the presence of a male to do this (of course, the eggs will be infertile). If this happens do not remove all the eggs as they are laid, but leave some with her to look after. Eventually she will tire of them, and then they can be discarded. If they are removed as she lays them, she will simply lay more than she would otherwise have done. This can place a great strain on her body, and could result in fatigue and illness.

You will find that no two parrots are quite the same, each displays its own unique character. Some are very affectionate, others quietly aloof. Some will welcome attention from anyone, others will restrict their attentions to family members, or even to a given sex, or person. This is why some owners will end up with a small collection. If you devote the needed time to your parrot, you will have a true companion for many years to come.

# Breeding Parrots

Successful breeding, even the most common of parrots, is an exciting experience that far surpasses merely owning them. It is an achievement that provides a special sense of gratification. It is also time and cost consuming. Merely reproducing the species with the freely available parrots has little merit, so the object is to try and improve the quality of these birds with each new generation. Conversely, in respect to other species, the ability to get the birds to reproduce at all could be considered a major achievement in parrot circles—thus, the number of challenges awaiting the parrot enthusiast are many.

Nothing breeds success like success. If you are a newcomer to bird breeding, I suggest that even if you would like to attempt to breed the more costly species, you first gain practical experience with the likes of budgerigars, cockatiels or lovebirds, each of which has a well established captive

Male and female Eclectus Parrot, *Eclectus roratus*. Of the parrot family, this is one of the easiest birds to sex. The male is of green coloration with an orange beak, and the female is of red and purple coloration.

Two very beautiful and somberly colored birds are the Bourke's Parakeet, *Neophema bourkii*, and the Elegant Parakeet, *Neophema elegans*.

breeding record. Armed with the knowledge gained, you can then progress to Australian parakeets, ringnecks, or other slightly more difficult species before tackling the more hard to breed parrots.

### GENERAL COMMENTS

Most species of parrots will need to be bred as single pairs if you wish to maximize the chances of success, while minimizing the risk of potentially fatal fights and nest plundering. Budgerigars, cockatiels, certain lovebirds, and a few selected parrots can be colony bred, but even when this is possible it is often preferred to breed parrots in pairs in order to have control over which birds (and thus colors) mate with which.

Aviary breeding is the ideal way to proceed with breeding attempts because this normally results in strong, vigorous chicks. However, most parrots that can be bred at all will also breed indoors if the conditions are favorable. Indeed, most small parrots are bred this way. Only breed birds that are in really fit condition, especially the hens, otherwise you may find many problems, such as egg binding, lack of eggs, or sickly chicks and so on.

The best breeding time is during the warmer months of April through September, though year 'round results are possible indoors where you are able to create artificial light and maintain suitable temperatures. Never attempt to over breed your birds because this will result in reduced clutch sizes, less robust chicks, and hens whose health will

suffer.

Before commencing a breeding program it is important to have sufficient extra cages or flights available to accommodate the chicks. Also, prepare breeding records so that you can document your results. Things such as the number of eggs, number of chicks, number that die and why, sexes (if these can be established), colors, and details of the feeding regimen should be recorded. The more data you have to refer back on, the more valuable this becomes as time goes by.

## ACQUIRING TRUE PAIRS

The first problem you may encounter in breeding parrots is that of obtaining a true pair of birds. Some species are dimorphic, meaning the sexes can be identified by their plumage colors, but in most species the sexes look alike. When you see an advertisement for a pair of a given species, it does not necessarily mean one of each sex, actually it means two birds. Even when you obtain a true pair, which will be advertised as such, this does not always mean that they will be compatible. The larger parrots especially, can be notoriously obstinate in

refusing a given mate, whom they may attack on sight.

The next level of pairs is thus a compatible pair. Here, the birds have proven to the seller they can live amicably together, but have never bred. Finally, the ideal state is a proven breeding pair. These will generally be the most expensive. As a rule of thumb you can work on the basis that the smaller parakeets and parrots will present fewer problems in "firing off" as breeding birds. With the large species, you may have to

Jandaya Conure chicks, *Aratinga jandaya*. Baby conures have a rapid growth rate. These chicks are approximately 4½ weeks old, and in another 6 weeks will be fully feathered and near full size.

The hand-rearing of birds, such as these Blue-streaked Lory chicks, *Eos reticulata*, is a difficult procedure. It should not be attempted unless one has a great deal of experience.

pair them up for a year or two before they will settle down to produce families—so do not expect things to happen rapidly just because you have included a nest box in their aviary.

The medium to larger parrots can be surgically sexed by your veterinarian saving you a lot of wasted time. Such birds are often so advertised. With the smaller and less expensive species, place three or more of them in a flight with nest boxes and hopefully they will pair off on their own. Once this has happened you must remove the unpaired birds and give the pairs their own accommodation. You could place temporary leg bands on the differing sexes, but most parrots are able to remove these with ease. Underwing tattooing, or microchip implants are modern ways to identify the sexes once these have been established.

Given the comments, with respect to larger parrots, you will appreciate

that once a proven pair has been established, it is unwise to split them up unless the situation demands this. Parrots are very loyal to their partners and pair bonds will invariably last the whole of their lives. This is as true of small species as of large ones, though breeders of the smaller species will often split pairs up each year because these will normally accept new partners more readily, which may be desired by the breeder.

In the wild, the Princess of Wales Parrot, *Polytelis alexandrae*, is said to breed in the hollows of trees usually close to river banks or creeks.

## NEST BOXES

It is well beyond the scope of this chapter to be able to discuss the individual nest box needs of the many parrot species, so what follows is an overview of these structures as an introduction. You should seek out specific information from specialized texts devoted to the species, or group of parrots, you plan to keep.

Most parrots in the wild utilize rotted branches or trunks of trees to fashion a nest. Some species, such as the Quaker Parakeet, build nests from twigs, while others, such as the Red-faced Lovebird, burrow into earth mounds. These are not typical for the parrot group of birds. For the majority of species a wooden nest box is the choice, with wooden barrels, hollowed logs, and their like being used by breeders of the large species. Generally, the nest box will be taller than it is wide, and is often referred to as a grandfather nest box, for the tall clocks of that name.

Baby Umbrella Cockatoo, *Cacatua alba.* Successful captive breeding of parrots often requires the the breeder to interfere. Occasionally, the parent birds will stop feeding the young or will begin to pick on them so much that death can occur.

Whatever nest box style is adopted, there are some comments that apply to all. The box should be very stoutly constructed using timber of at least 1 in (2.5 cm) thickness if it is for use in an outside aviary or is for indoor use for any but the smaller parrot species. This helps to maintain a constant temperature, which thin wood will not do. Further, thin wood will not last long with most parrot species.

The inner dimensions of the nest box will reflect the species. A beginner's

common error is to make this too large. As a guide, if a square shape is used, its width should be just a little longer than the beak to rump size of the bird—you do not need to consider the tail length of longtailed species. The height of the nest box will normally be anywhere from fifty percent to three times the width, depending on the species.

The outdoor nest box should have a roof that extends beyond the box walls so that these are protected from rain and strong sunlight. There must be an entrance hole to the nest box, having a landing perch just below it. The hole need not be large, but indeed should be a snug fit for the species in question. The hen will then enlarge this to her satisfaction. It can be a square or round hole. Many breeders place the hole in a central position a few inches below the roof, however, parrots seem to prefer it placed to one side so that the actual nest is in darkness.

If a tall box is used, it will need a ladder type device on its inner surface, on the hole side. This will enable the hen to easily climb out. Some breeders staple weld wire on the inner edge, but I prefer to nail struts of timber as

The male Eastern Rosella, *Platycercus eximius*, is much more vividly colored than the female. A female exhibits the same coloration, only much paler.

there is no risk a hen or chick could get their claws or ring entangled in the weld wire. By assembling the nest box with screws, it can be taken apart after each season, repaired, and thoroughly disinfected—ready for the next season. This is most important because you do not want any risk of mite infestation in the nest box.

In order to safeguard the box base from rotting caused by urine seeping into the wood—or from the hen gnawing at the base, it is useful to place a thick piece of wood as a false floor in the box. If this is slightly hollowed it will help retain the eggs in the center of the box. These concaves can be purchased for the nest boxes of small species, such as budgerigars. A further

addition to a nest box can be a sliding tray beneath the floor, which can be drilled with a few very small holes that will be beneath the concave of the box. Water can be placed into the tray, which will help maintain a good humidity level in the nest. This can be very important during very hot weather, especially for the tropical parrots.

In order to facilitate nest inspection, the roof of the nest box can be hinged, or you can place a hinged door on the back or side walls. This should be at a height that will not result in the chicks falling out when it is opened. The nest box can be placed either in the shelter, under a protected part of the aviary, in the outside flight, or on the outside of a cage if you plan to breed in a bird room. If situated on the outside, you will need to make a hole in the side wall of wooden cages, or cut a suitable hole in the mesh front of a cage that is part of a block. This is the most popular method, and cage fronts can be purchased that already feature holes ready to take a nest box.

If you should attempt colony breeding with budgerigars, cockatiels, or other species that will breed in this manner, you must hang more boxes than there are pairs of birds. This gives them a choice of sites. Once the birds have chosen a box, the spares can be removed. To minimize squabbling, place the boxes at the same height. With individual pairs you can again hang two or three boxes in different sites so they can pick the one they prefer. You might even offer them a choice of nest box styles.

If a pair of birds shows no interest in the sites you chose, try other sites. If a pair of parrots does not like the nest box site, they will not breed; this can often be the sole reason for non-production. Although most species prefer boxes placed high in the aviary, and in a protected and discreet position, some may prefer a lower box, so always consider this aspect. Some species will only need the nest box during the breeding period, in which case it can be placed into the aviary a few weeks before you hope the pair will go to nest. Other species will roost in their boxes during the non-breeding period, so their boxes can be left in position year 'round (but removed periodically for thorough cleaning).

From the foregoing you will understand that nest

**Facing page:** Birds that get on well with each other can be housed together in the same aviary. If breeding is intended, place more nest boxes in the cage than pairs of birds to prevent squabbling.

Female Eclectus Parrot, *Eclectus roratus*. The feathers of the Eclectus are very fine and upon viewing this bird for the first time, one may think them to be hair-like.

box style and siting are crucial for most species. However, some pairs are so keen to reproduce that they will nest almost anywhere—even in a tray on the aviary or cage floor. You should be so lucky as to own such pairs, so make every effort to provide the best nesting facilities you can. The floor covering of the nest box will reflect the species. For some parrots it need only be sparse, for others quite a generous layer. It can be a few twigs, granulated paper, peat, or commercial nesting material from your pet shop.

**BREEDING DATA**

Once a pair of parrots has mated, generally it is the hen that incubates the eggs. The cock will often roost on the nest box, or on a nearby perch. The notable exception to this rule is the cockatoos, where both parents share the incubation duties. All parrot eggs are white, and the size of the clutch is influenced by numerous factors. These include the species, the age of the pair, and the ambient temperature (which affects the fertilization rate). The potential range of a clutch can be from 1-9, with an average in the popular smaller species of about 3-5. Eggs are laid on alternate days in the small species, but the interval between eggs can be longer with the large parrots. The hen may commence "sitting" to incubate the eggs after the first egg is laid, or she may wait until the second or third egg has been produced. The mortality rate of both embryo and chicks can be quite high in this group of birds, as can the number of infertile eggs. This is not because the birds are in any way less able to breed than other bird groups, but because in many instances breeder error or mismanagement is a factor to a greater or lesser degree. For example, either of a pair may not be in breeding condition, or the nest box will be inadequate in some way. The temperature and humidity within the nest may fluctuate too much, or the breeder will stress the parents by interfering (inspecting the nest) too often.

The Turquoise Grass Parakeet, *Neophema pulchella*, is a typical ground feeding bird that spends a great deal of time climbing among shrubbery.

The duration of incubation will range from a minimum of about 17 days in budgerigars and cockatiels, to as long as 30 days in the larger parrots from Grey Parrots to cockatoos. The period the chicks will spend in the nest is equally variable, from as little as four weeks in the small parakeets, to as long as three months in Grey Parrots, macaws, and lorikeets. Most of the popular parakeets and parrots will spend from 5-9 weeks in the nest. When they leave this they are said to be of fledgling age.

Even before a clutch of chicks leaves the nest the hen may commence to lay a second round of eggs. In such cases the cock will invariably continue to feed the chicks and the hen until the chicks are removed to a nursery cage or aviary. In some species, one or both of the parents may attack the youngsters still around the nest when the pair is ready to start a second clutch of eggs. You must therefore be very observant of such times and remove the chicks once you feel they are established enough to feed themselves. Never allow chicks to go to new homes until you are totally sure they are feeding well on their own.

It is never wise to allow your parrots to continually breed. This remark is targeted toward popular parrots such as budgerigars, cockatiels, lovebirds, and those parakeets which are ready breeders. When they have reared three or four clutches they should be given time to recuperate for the following season. To prevent them from breeding, remove the nest box. If they are a species that roosts in the nest, you should remove all nesting material. If all else fails, split the pair up, but house them in adjacent cages where they can still see and sit close to each other if the same pair is to breed next season.

If after reading this brief introduction to this subject you decide you would like to breed parrots, I suggest you seek out more detailed information. Apart from specific data on your chosen parrots, it should also discuss aspects such as egg storage, breeding problems, incubators, leg banding, chick rearing, and fostering eggs or chicks. In the case of budgerigars, cockatiels, lovebirds, and certain parakeets, you would also gain considerably by studying basic genetics and its application to color mutations in particular.

**Facing page:** Eclectus Parrot chicks, *Eclectus roratus.* Chicks of the same nest will often huddle together, usually for warmth and security. After the chicks mature a little, they will begin to explore their surroundings on their own.

Sun Conures, *Aratinga solstitialis,* adult and immature. As youngsters mature, the yellow on the wing coverts becomes more extensive.

# Health Care

The smaller size of the Monk Parakeet, *Myiopsitta monachus*, appeals to people who would like to have a parrot, but cannot accomodate one with the required space.

The subject of diseases and conditions that could afflict your parrot is such that it could, and does, take up entire volumes. Here we will review management techniques that will greatly reduce the chance that your bird will become ill. The owner with a single pet parrot in the home is largely protected from many of the health hazards known to afflict birds, so the text is directed essentially towards the multi-parrot owner and breeder. However, most of what follows has application even to the single bird owner.

## ROUTINE HYGIENE

Possibly because it is such an obvious area of management, it is not always appreciated just how important routine hygiene is in avian husbandry. Indeed, it would be true to say that most diseases that arrive in an owner's home or breeding room do so because of a lack of hygiene in one of its many forms. The following are key areas to attend to without fail:

1. Always wash your hands before and after handling *each* of your parrots.

2. Wash feed and water containers on a regular basis—daily is the ideal, but certainly every three days. Be sure the feed and water dishes are placed back in the same cage they came from. Number the cages and the feeders.

3. Discard any feeding utensils and pots that become cracked, chipped, or badly scratched.

Always keep spares on hand for this.

4. Be very sure to keep perches clean, and to replace them once the parrots have nibbled them beyond the point where they are not easily cleaned. Your birds will constantly rub their beaks on the perches, and this is a prime way pathogens (disease causing organisms) are able to transfer from one bird to another. Cage bars should also be kept in a very clean state for the same reason.

5. Food must be stored in airtight containers and kept in a dark, dry place. There must never be any chance that mice or rats can feed on them, nor wild bird droppings can fall in them. Feed only the best seeds and fresh foods. Always rinse green foods before giving them to your birds.

6. Never allow garden refuse to be piled up anywhere near your aviaries. It could be the source of all manner of diseases. Likewise, when you sweep up your breeding room each day make sure the debris is removed from the room and burnt, or otherwise disposed of.

7. Use disposable, surgical, or thin rubber gloves when handling sick birds.

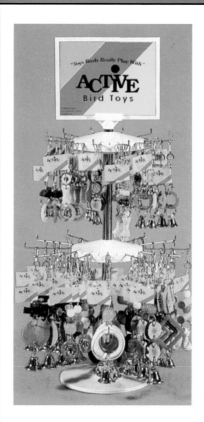

An assortment of Active Bird Toys can be found on display at your local pet shop. It may be hard to choose just one for your pet!

8. Maintain a strict schedule of aviary and bird room cleaning. This should be done at least once per week, and more often if a large number of birds are in your collection. If you find you are not coping with routine hygiene due to lack of time, reduce the number of birds you keep, or get help.

## QUARANTINE

After your first parrot has been acquired, all further additions should be quarantined away from the rest of your stock—and from other pets you may keep. The suggested

Green-cheeked Amazon, *Amazona viridigenalis*. Parrots enjoy spending time away from their cage with their owner. Normally, when first allowed out of its cage the bird will spend a few minutes stretching its wings before it plays with its owner.

isolation period is 14-21 days, which is generally sufficient for any incubating disease to manifest itself. During this period you can carefully monitor the feeding habits of new arrivals, as well as routinely treat the birds for both para-sites (such as mites) and for worms. The best preparations for these can be obtained from your veterinarian. As a matter of policy, worm all breeding birds just prior to the season.

## KNOW YOUR PARROTS

The first indications of ill health, possibly the only ones, may be behavioral changes. To recognize these you must know your birds on an individual basis. An ill bird may show reduced interest in food, water, or both. It may sit hunched at one end of its perch, or even flutter to the corner of its cage.

Clinical signs of ill health have been discussed earlier. Basically, any appearance in your bird that does not suggest super condition is the result of a problem.

## BE PREPARED FOR ILLNESS

Once you begin to gather a small collection of parrots, you must assume that sooner or later one or more of these will become ill. All too often when problems manifest themselves novice breeders are totally unprepared for the situation. You need to purchase an infrared lamp, and have an isolation cage ready. You could purchase a commercial hospital cage, but for most parrots one fashioned by yourself will be every bit as good, and possibly better for the larger species.

The cage should be of generous size in its length, and be fitted with two low perches. It could be made using coated timber so it is easily disinfected after each use. Alternatively, you could line a stock cage with Plexiglas or give it a generous coating with a washable paint (non-lead based). The lamp should be wired through a thermostat so the temperature can be controlled. It can be mounted about 6 in (15 cm) in front of the cage, at one end. Having the lamp at one end enables the bird to move away from the heat source if it finds it becoming uncomfortable as it gets better.

A protected dish of water (separate from the drinking water) can be placed such that it will maintain the humidity level in the cage. Likewise, two protected thermometers (one at each end) should be a feature of a homemade hospital cage. Place the cage in a quiet spot and well away from the main stock. The temperature needed will be 85-90°F (29-32°C). This will normally cope with minor chills, shock, and other non-specific complaints. More serious diseases will

of course require the treatment of modern drugs prescribed after consultation with your vet.

If your vet wishes to have you bring in a sick parrot that has been subjected to heat treatment, be very sure it is transported in a well protected cage so there is no risk of it chilling. After heat treatment, a recovered bird should not be immediately returned to its aviary. You must acclimatize it over a number of days by reducing the heat in the cage until it is back to room

Small as they may be, only measuring 9in (22.5cm) long, the Senegal Parrot, *Poicephalus senegalus*, can still prove to be very destructive.

temperature. If the outside weather is inclement, do not return it to an outdoor aviary at that time.

**PROMPT ACTION**

A bird can go downhill very rapidly once it has contracted an illness. It is vital that you react promptly once you sense that something is amiss. Indecision may cost your parrot its life. First, isolate the bird, then call your vet. If you cannot contact your vet at that time, supply heat treatment. Be sure water is freely available and maintain the food supply pending advice from your vet. Note carefully the clinical or other signs of ill health, and all related matters. These will include how long the bird has been owned, its source, its diet, the state of its feces, recent illnesses, and as much other information as you can document for the vet.

Modern treatments may first require blood or fecal samples after which there are a range of antibiotics that can be prescribed. Some of these may be administered via the water, fruits, orally, or by injection, depending on the size of the bird. Other treatments may be via direct application of ointments, or surgery, again depending on the size of the bird and the problem. In the event a bird dies without displaying clinical signs, you are strongly advised to have your vet conduct an autopsy to try and identify the cause—it may save other valuable parrots in your collection.

Preventive medicine is by far your most powerful weapon in the fight against disease. Devote your efforts to this, rather than studying the diseases, most of which you will not be able to diagnose without microscopy. In any event, only a vet can know which treatments are best, their likely side effects, how long they should be administered for, and so on.

Treatments for respiratory ailments as well as other types of medication are available from your local pet shop. Photo courtesy of Rolf C. Hagen Corp.

HAGEN

COLD & RESPIRATORY AID

For Birds

- Relieves colds and bronchial disorders
- Reduces sneezing and nasal discharges
- Aids breathing
(Directions on back panel)

TRAITEMENT CONTRE LE RHUME ET LES AFFECTIONS RESPIRATOIRES

Chez les oiseaux

- Soulage le rhume et les affections bronchiques
- Réduit l'éternuement et l'écoulement nasal
- Facilite la respiration
(Mode d'emploi au verso)

HAGEN

COLD AID
for Birds
TRAITEMENT POUR
LE RHUME
pour Oiseaux

Net contents 1 fl. oz.
Contenu net 30 ml

Art. B-2142

# Popular Parrot Species

Of the approximately 330 parrot species only relatively few can be regarded as being highly popular. Some are not seen in collections, while many are only rarely bred in captivity. In this chapter we will look at those most likely to be available from your local pet store, or in the aviaries of breeders, plus a few that are less commonly available. Some are discussed as individual species, others as part of a natural group of species.

When discussing the nature and compatibility of any parrot you must always allow for the individuals that do not fit the accepted norm for the species. For example, cockatiels are the most endearing of parrots that are very safe with even small finches in mixed collections. There is, however, always the odd rogue that may have been poorly bred, or made

Cinnamon Whiteface Cockatiel, *Nymphicus hollandicus.* There are many mutations of cockatiels available. Some, like this Cinnamon Whiteface are not as commonly seen as others.

nervous at some point in its life. Conversely, there are large parrots that have proved very compatible with smaller birds in spite of the fact that such combinations are not recommended. Also, bear in mind that the nature of a bird can change dramatically during the breeding period. A normally peaceful parrot in a mixed bird collection can become a positive danger to the other birds at this time.

Always judge parrots individually, not solely based on what books say they should be like.

**BUDGERIGAR**
(*Melopsittacus undulatus*)
    This little Australian grass parakeet has probably introduced more people to the hobby of bird keeping than any other

The basic coloration of the Salmon-crested Cockatoo, *Cacatua moluccensis*, also known as the Moluccan Cockatoo, is a light peach with much yellow diffusion, especially under the wings.

avian. It makes a delightful pet, and is the most bred and exhibited parrot in the world. It is so well known that a description is not needed. Budgies can be bred in pairs, or in a colony system. They are also quite safe in mixed bird collections if housed with other peaceful species. They are best sexed during the breeding period when the cere of the male is blue while that of the female is brown. Young, straight from the nest juveniles are duller in color than the adults, have barring on their heads, and a gray iris.

Easily hand tamed, the cocks can make excellent talking birds, though only the owner may be able to discern all of their words. The range of colors in this species is greater than in any other bird thanks to the many color mutations that can be combined to create an almost indefinite range of shades and patterns. An ideal first time parrot for any owner, and especially recommended to the novice breeder. Price range is from a few dollars to quite high prices for quality exhibition stock in the rarer mutations.

## COCKATIEL
### (*Nymphicus hollandicus*)

To this author, and possibly to many other parrot enthusiasts, the cockatiel has to be the best all around parrot for the breeder or the pet owner to commence with— maybe even ahead of the ubiquitous budgerigar on account of its larger size. In length, this Australian relative of the cockatoo reaches about 13 in (33 cm). With its gray and white plumage, orange cheek spots, and yellow crest, it is an imposing bird. In its lutino mutational form it is quite stunning. There are a number of other color mutations as well.

Sun Conure, *Aratinga solstitialis.* Conures enjoy being handled. They tame fairly easy and prove to be very affectionate.

The Barred Parakeet, *Bolborhynchus lineola*, like many other parrots, naturally gnaws upon wood in the wild. It is advisable to include many chew toys in your bird's cage to accommodate this need.

**Facing page:** The Black-headed Caique, *Pionites melanocephala*, is a very lively species. They must be provided with adequate branches to gnaw upon because of their rather destructive nature.

The hen is a duller version of the cock, and the underside of her tail is gray barred with yellow, compared with the dark gray to black of the male. Sexing can be difficult in some of the mutational color forms. Youngsters resemble the hen. The cocks can learn a few words and have their own very pleasant whistle.

Obtain hand-reared babies, or those straight from the nest. Even adults of this species can be hand tamed with great patience. Like the budgie, they can be bred in pairs, in a colony, or in a mixed bird collection where they are extremely peaceful and safe with even the smallest of finches. They are not noisy aviary birds, so will not offend your neighbors. Pet cockatiels are truly delightful and gentle parrots, and they only have a small beak. They make superb exhibition and breeding propositions. Somewhat more costly than the budgerigar, they can range to quite expensive for valuable breeding pairs of the most sought after mutations. Check out all the varieties before making your choice.

**LOVEBIRDS**
(Genus *Agapornis*)

The common name of this group of little African parrots is derived from the fact that pairs will sit close to each other and indulge in mutual preening. However, do not let this fool you into thinking they will make nice residents in a mixed aviary. Their size belies their very often belligerent nature, which verges on murderous when they are breeding! Although small, ranging from 5–6½ in (13–16.5 cm), they have large beaks for their size and are tough little parrots. If in mixed aviaries, only house with larger birds which are able to defend themselves well.

There are nine lovebird species, but one of these is not available to aviculture. Of the remaining eight, three are very popular, the others much less so. The Peach-faced Lovebird (*Agapornis roseicollis*) is by far the most commonly available, and is also seen in a number of color mutations. This makes it a popular choice with color breeders and exhibitors. The other two species normally available in pet shops are the Masked Lovebird (*Agapornis personata*) and the Fischer's Lovebird (*Agapornis fischeri*). Both of these also have mutational color forms that are very striking.

Hand-reared or straight from the nest babies can be charming little companions. Adults will

not tame easily, and are capable of inflicting quite a hard bite for their size, so only youngsters are advised as pets. The basic plumage colors are green with pink, orange, red, black, yellow, or gray according to the

species. In the three species mentioned, the sexes cannot be differentiated from external appearance, which makes obtaining breeding pairs more difficult. They are an excellent choice for the novice breeder, and are very popular exhibition birds. Prices are modest in the popular species (good exhibition birds will cost you a lot more), and variable in the other species according to availability. This tends to fluctuate, but cost is rarely low these days in comparison to past years when importations were much more numerous.

Looking very similar to the lovebirds are the parrotlets of South America (genus *Forpus*). These are delightful little parrots whose basic colors are green with some yellow, blue, and gray according to species. They make excellent breeding birds, but are far less available than lovebirds these days.

Yet another group of parrots superficially similar to the lovebirds are the hanging parrots of the genus *Loriculus*. They are native to Asia and the Pacific Islands. They are not at all aggressive, and may even be kept in planted aviaries. These are more costly to purchase, and not that readily available.

The Maroon-bellied Conure, *Pyrrhura frontalis*, does not have a very raucous voice as most other conure species.

## LONGTAILED ASIATIC PARAKEETS

In past years a number of the longtailed parrots of Asia were extremely inexpensive to purchase and therefore were rarely bred. Times have changed, and they are much more costly these days. A number of the popular species will make delightful pets and good aviary birds, though not all experts will agree on their suitability as pets. This author has kept a number of these as pets and found them very affectionate, but they must be given plenty of time out of their cage. Being larger birds than those so far discussed, they can be more destructive and noisier, so do bear this in mind. However, in terms of noise they still do not compare with the larger parrots nor with their size wise counterparts of South America to be discussed later.

The least expensive of this group of birds is the Rose-ringd Parakeet (*Psittacula krameri*), so named for the narrow band of black and red that encircles the under beak and neck of the males. They are otherwise green birds with red beaks. Extremely elegant, they reach a length of about 15.7 in (40 cm). The lutino (yellow) and the

blue mutational color forms are quite breathtaking, but very costly. There is also an African Parakeet which is of the same species, but slightly smaller.

More colorful, though a little less elegant due to its larger head size and shorter tail, is the Moustached Parakeet (*Psittacula alexandri*). This bird has a broad black moustache and a narrow black frontal band across its forehead. The chest is a delicate pink. The beak of the male is red, that of the female black. It is slightly smaller in length

The preening action of this Hyacinth Macaw, *Anodorhynchus hyacinthinus*, toward this Green-winged Macaw, *Ara chloroptera*, helps to reinforce the bond between two birds.

Pacific Parrotlet, *Forpus coelestis*. These small members of the parrot family are ideal choices for pets where space is limited.

than the previous parakeets.

An extremely beautiful parrot in this group is the Plum-headed Parakeet (*Psittacula cyanocephala*). The head of the male is a deep plum color, that of the female being a more sober blue-gray with a hint of pink. The male has a black neck ring which is bordered by a blue-green color. The body is green with a lighter shade on the chest, and the central tail feathers are blue. A maroon patch on the upper wing coverts completes this magnificent species.

The largest of the Asiatic parakeets is the

Alexandrine Parakeet (*Psittacula eupatria*). This parrot may reach 24 in (60 cm) in length. It sports a large red beak and is colored similar to the Rose-ringed Parakeet, but easily distinguished from it by its more massive head and greater size. Lutino and blue mutations are magnificent—but very costly.

The Derbyan Parakeet (*Psittacula derbiana*) is a very handsome bird which has a lilac-mauve chest, a blue head broken up by a frontal band of black from eye to eye, and a large area of black around the throat. The beak of the male is red, that of the female black. Unfortunately, it is one of the more noisy parakeets of this group.

The Long-tailed Parakeet (*Psittacula longicauda*) will complete the birds we will consider of the *Psittacula* genus. It has a length of around 16 in (41 cm), and features a broad area of rose-orange-red below the green cap of the head. This is bounded by a black moustache, which is dark green in the female. The beak is red in the male and brown in the female.

The Asiatic parakeets make an ideal group of birds for a breeder to specialize in, as do many of the Australian parakeets. They can be more of a challenge and rather expenisve, but their cost these days justifies the efforts needed to establish breeding pairs.

## AFRICAN PARROTS
Of all the world's parrots few are so well known as pets as the number native to Africa. The king among these is undoubtedly the Grey Parrot (*Psittacus erithacus*), whose

power of mimicry is almost legendary. This entirely gray bird features a bare area of skin around its eyes, has a short red tail, and the head and neck feathers display a scalloped effect. Length is in the order of 13 in (33 cm). It cannot be confused with any other parrot.

One of the most beautifully colored of the conures, the Sun Conure, *Aratinga solstitialis*, is often one of the most favored.

The Grey Parrot is so good at mimicry that it can faithfully reproduce the sound of a squeaking door, the noise of a hammer, or the whistling of a kettle, as readily as it can the human voice or the song of a bird. There are thus mixed blessings with such talents! If you want a pet Grey, you must purchase a hand-reared or very young baby; wild caught adults are almost impossible to tame satisfactorily. Possibly more so than with comparable parrots, the Greys can show decided preferences for the people they attach themselves to.

The Senegal Parrot (*Poicephalus senegalus*) is a bit smaller than the Grey Parrot, being 10 in (25 cm). The main features of this

Moustached Parakeet, *Psittacula alexandri fasciata*. The coloring of some parrots is so defined that even an artist painting a picture could not produce such beauty.

bird are its gray head, black beak, and orange-yellow chest and underparts. Some people find it a rather aggressive looking bird. But looks are deceptive and it makes a very fine pet; ranking among the best if obtained as a baby.

Jardine's Parrot (*Poicephalus gulielmi*) is an attractive bird with splashes of orange on its forehead and wing shoulders. It has a bare eye ring, large black beak, and is about 12 in (30 cm) in length. Another African parrot that is available from time to time is the Meyer's Parrot (*Poicephalus meyeri*) which, like the Senegal, has a gray hood.

### AUSTRALIAN PARAKEETS

Although Australians are unable, in many instances, to obtain examples of parrots from other countries (imports being banned since 1959), they are blessed with having access to some of the most spectacular parrots in the world that are native to their country. These are the cockatoos and the numerous parakeets. While many of the parakeets are kept as pets in Australia, and are highly regarded, these birds are traditionally seen only in aviaries in Europe and the USA. They are much more popular in Europe than in the USA, but are continually adding devotees in the New World.

As aviary birds they have few, if any, peers as a group. The colors seen in the species are often quite spectacular, many are very reliable breeders, and they do not have the raucous voices of their South

Major Mitchell's Cockatoo, *Cacatua leadbeateri*, is a very beautiful bird because of its uniquely colored crest, and its light pastel body color.

Crimson Rosella, *Platycercus elegans.* Rosellas have a very large wing span, and are very active birds. It is best to house these birds in either large cages or aviaries so that the proper amount of exercise can be attained.

American counterparts. Further, they are rarely destructive to their aviaries, so have just about every attribute you could want.

Of the smaller species the Scarlet-chested (*Neophema splendida*), at about 8 in (19 cm) is aptly named. It is quite gorgeous, the male has a deep blue face and blue on the wing butts. The chest is scarlet giving way to yellow on the underparts. The hen lacks the scarlet, and is also paler in her other colors. The rest of the plumage is basically green. Not quite as spectacular, but still a very attractively colored bird, is the Turquoise (*Neophema pulchella*). It has blue on the head and wings, the chest is a yellow color, and there are small patches of red in the wings. Another small grass parakeet that has great beauty is the Elegant (*Neophema elegans*), this bird being just slightly larger than the previous two.

Moving up in cost and size, if you like red you will adore the Crimson Rosella (*Platycercus elegans*) which is 14 in (36 cm) long. This avian jewel is predominantly a red and blue bird, and is also known as the Pennant's Parakeet. The wide tails of the Rosellas gives rise to their other common name of broadtails. For really striking colors few parrots can match the Gold-mantled, Red, or Eastern Rosella (*Platycercus eximius*). This 12 in (30 cm) parakeet includes red, white, blue, yellow, black, and green in its plumage, so always commands attention when seen for the first time. If its vivid colors are not enough, it is also the most easily bred of the larger parakeets, so is modest in cost for such grandeur. Other Rosellas

include the Yellow (*Platycercus flaveolus*),which has much yellow on it as its name would suggest. The Green Rosella (*Platycercus caledonicus*) is somber by comparison to the others just described, yet is a very colorful bird with its green and yellow plumage splashed with red and blue. It remains rather uncommon compared to other Australasian parakeets (actually it is from Tasmania). More Australian jewels in the parrot world include the Regent Parrot (*Polytelis*

The Bourke's Parakeet, *Neophema bourkii*, has very beautiful, soft coloring that is not as easily seen on a perched bird as it is on one that has its wings extended during flight.

The Grey-cheeked Parakeet, *Brotogeris pyrrhopterus*, is a very comical little bird that enjoys spending time away from its cage.

*anthopeplus*), Superb (*Polytelis swainsonii*), Princess of Wales (*Polytelis alexandrae*), and the Golden-shouldered (*Psephotus chrysopterygius*), to name but a few.

Very common (thus modest in price) are the Bourke's (*Neophema bourkii*), the Blue-winged (*Neophema chrysostoma*), and the Red-rumped (*Psephotus haematonotus*). There are numerous color mutations of these birds

which are rather expensive. If you are thinking of breeding any of these parakeets in your aviary, do yourself a great favor and review all of the Australian species.

**AMAZON PARROTS**
Turning from aviary birds to those of the New World which are kept more as pets than for breeding, the amazon parrots of South America have long been firm favorites. Many are now being domestically bred, especially in the USA, to supply the waiting pet market. Their great charm lies in their amusing antics, lively personalities, and good ability to talk, though not to the standard of the Grey Parrot. The basic color is green with variable splashes of yellow, blue, or red according to the species.

The down side of these birds is that they are prone to periodic outbursts of very high pitched screeching. This limits them from a breeding viewpoint in outdoor aviaries if you have close neighbors. Three of the more popular species are the Blue-fronted (*Amazona aestiva*) at 14 in (36 cm), which actually has little blue on its head, this being mainly yellow, the Orange-winged (*Amazona amazonica*), a slightly smaller bird with much blue over its crown, and the Yellow-corwned (*Amazona ochrocephala*). Each of these can be very talented talkers, especially the Blue-fronted and the Double Yellow-headed race of the yellow crowns.

The largest of the Amazons is the rather soberly colored Mealy (*Amazona farinosa*) which can exceed 15 in (38 cm). In contrast the Green-cheeked, or Mexican Red-headed Amazon, is vividly colored with a bright red crown, light green cheeks and horn colored beak. It is a very popular bird in the USA, but less so in Britain.

**NEW WORLD PARAKEETS**

The South and Central American parakeets are a very large group of parrots, some of which are popular both as pets and aviary breeding birds. A few are very colorful, but most, like the amazon parrots, are basically green with various colored splashes on their head or wings. Many of the neotropical parakeets can make extremely confiding pets if acquired at a young age. As aviary inhabitants their main drawback, apart from lack of color, is their rather harsh voice, which they are prone to use quite a bit at times. Unlike the Australian parakeets, those from the neotropics will require much more variety in their diets. They will consume more fruits for example, as well as a wider range of seeds, so are totally different than the Australian species in respect to the diet they will accept.

Conures (genus *Aratinga*) are another group of parrots, less expensive than those belonging to the amazon group. Three

The Green-cheeked Amazon, *Amazona viridigenalis*, is a very lively bird that can raise its shrill voice very loudly, particularly in the morning and evening hours.

Barred Parakeet, *Bolborhynchus lineola.* Parrots truly love to be destructive. Toys and accessories made of rope and wood prove great fun for them to demolish.

outstandingly beautiful and popular conures are the Jandaya (*Aratinga jandaya*), the Sun (*Aratinga solstitialis*), and the Queen of Bavaria or Golden (*Aratinga guarouba*). Each of these is predominantly yellow with a black beak. They are 12-14 in (30-36 cm) in length depending on the species.

Probably one of the best known conures is the Nanday (*Nandayus nenday*) with its black hood and beak and blue chest. It is a proven breeder and can be colony bred. It also makes a very nice pet. It has a length of about 12 in (31 cm).

Much smaller at 9½ in (24 cm), but very popular in the USA, is the Orange-fronted Conure (*Aratinga canicularis*). It is similar to the Gold-crowned Conure, which it is often mistaken for. The Gold-crowned has a black beak and the Orange-fronted's is horn colored. Both have orange foreheads with an area of dusky blue behind this.

One of the least costly of the neotropical parakeets is the Quaker or Monk Parakeet (*Myiopsitta monachus*). This 12 in (30 cm) parrot has impressive plumage in green with a gray-white forehead, throat, and chest. The beak is horn yellow. It will colony breed with no problems, its drawbacks are its voice and destructive habits to woodwork in the aviary. Young

Quakers make very nice pets, so are a good option to consider, and they may learn a few words.

**PIONUS PARROTS**

The genus *Pionus* contains a number of neotropical parrots that have interest to both breeders and pet owners. Pet owners in particular might find certain of these parrots superior to the amazons because they are quieter.

Scaly-headed Parrot (*Pionus maximiliani*) reaches 12 in (30 cm) in length and is pleasingly colored with an area of blue on its throat, a red tail, and white eye-ring. The White-capped Parrot (*Pionus senilis*) is much smaller at 9½ in (24 cm), and sports a white cap on its head, and a white area on its throat. Possibly

Sun Conure, *Aratinga solstitialis*. The small size, cheerful personalities, and beautiful colors of a conure are very good reasons to keep them as pets.

**Facing page:** Chattering Lory, *Lorius garrulus*. Lories are very playful birds. They are very inquisitive creatures that enjoy playing games with their owners.

The Blue-headed Parrot, *Pionus menstruus*, is a medium sized parrot with a great deal of personality. It is stockier than the conures and not as large as the macaws, making it a nice size bird to handle.

the most popular of this genus is the Blue-headed Parrot (*Pionus menstruus*) which has a length of 11 in (28 cm). The blue head extends down the neck which becomes reddish on the throat. The beak is black and there are black ear coverts.

## CAIQUES

There are just two Caique species and both make very desirable pets in spite of their rather noisy voice and destructive to woodwork beaks. They have a length of 9 in (23 cm) so are a nice size. Their personality is of the highest order. They display their obvious intelligence with a zest for mischief and are always amusing and affectionate if purchased as babies. There is a Black-headed species (*Pionites melanocephala*) which has a yellow throat and neck over a white chest

and abdomen. The legs are yellow, the beak is black, and the rest of the plumage is green, making it a very distinctive bird. The White-bellied (*Pionites leucogaster*) has a yellow cape to the head and neck, and a horn colored beak. Otherwise it is similar to the Black-headed Caique.

## LORIES AND LORIKEETS

This group of Australasian parrots has two outstanding features—their vivid colors and their playfulness. They differ from other parrots in that they require nectar as an essential part of their diet. They can be rather messy birds, which is their singular drawback. Only consider these as pets after both careful thought, and a genuine willingness to devote a lot of extra attention to their diet, general cleaning, and the special caging is agreed upon. Some birds of this species can be obtained at very modest costs for aviary breeding, and given their spectacular colors they must be one of the bargains of the parrot world to those prepared to devote time to them.

## COCKATOOS AND MACAWS

Cockatoos hail from Australasia, while Macaws are neotropical. Both

groups of birds are of course quite stunning, either because of their size or their colors. The smaller macaws, such as the Red-shouldered (*Ara nobilis*) and the Chestnut-fronted (*Ara severa*) are relatively modest in cost. The larger and very colorful Blue and

Chestnut-fronted Macaw, *Ara severa*. Parrots seem to never get enough of exercising. They enjoy being away from the confines of a cage for as long of a period of time that they can be.

Gold (*Ara ararauna*) or the Scarlet (*Ara macao*), are much more costly, especially for hand-reared babies. Probably the most costly and gorgeous macaw available is the Hyacinth Macaw, which is an entirely cobalt blue bird with a yellow eye-ring.

Cockatoos are probably the most interestingly beautiful group of parrots. Many species are mostly white and sport erectile crests of various lengths. There are 17 species of cockatoos that range in size.

In general, I would not advise a first time parrot owner to obtain even a tame cockatoo or macaw. They have powerful beaks which can wreak havoc in the average home. They also have ear shattering voices that can be heard far away, which may not endear you to neighbors. They require a great deal of time devoted to them, even the small species, and the cost of their housing can be considerable. Gain experience with other, smaller parrots first, and this may tell you whether you would still want one of these larger birds, or would prefer to admire, but not keep them.

# SUGGESTED READING

T.F.H. offers the most comprehensive selections of books dealing with pet birds. A selection of significant titles is presented here; they and the thousands of other animal books published by T.F.H. are available at the same place you bought this one, or write to us for a free catalog.

T.F.H. Publications
One T.F.H. Plaza
Third & Union Avenues
Neptune, NJ 07753

# INDEX

Page numbers in boldface **refer to illustrations.**

# THE
# SOUTHERN WAY

## CONTENTS

© Kevin Robertson (Noodle Books) and the various contributors 2014
ISBN 978-1-909328-26-6
First published in 2014 by Kevin Robertson
under the **NOODLE BOOKS** imprint
PO Box 279
Corhampton
SOUTHAMPTON
SO32 3ZX
www.noodlebooks.co.uk
editorial@thesouthernway.co.uk

Printed in England by
Berforts Information Press Ltd.

***Above*** - *The Wallis collection continues to reveal surprises. We had already scanned this image but with the negative packet revealing nothing in the way of location or image detail. Then under our 'Wallis odds' file we came across the same image but this time scanned from (one of the very few) contact prints and with detail written on the reverse. "Redhill 'B' cabin: new down starting signal and route indicator" - the latter is the mechanical 'half-moon' device on the supporting cross girder, quite fascinating! The ladder crossing is also worthy of study, complete with its curved check-rails. (Readers will be pleased to learn a second 'Southern Infrastructure' with views from the collection is planned for the autumn, see advert! Also for the autumn is 'Great Western Infrastructure', again solely with images from the same archive.)*

# Editorial

I am glad I am not alone in craving nostalgia. Not just railway but to be perfectly honest, almost everything I recall from years ago, witnessed or wish I had witnessed. That said I also relish my 21st century comforts!

Clearly I am not alone in this vision as it appears there are numerous amongst us who share the same perspective. One of these is a man called Antony Hemens and who may perhaps best be described (if he will forgive me) as having not just a nostalgia for but more of a passion for his favourite railway subject, in his case the lines around Midhurst. Antony is also in an ideal geographical position to foster that passion, living in Sussex and so on-hand to notice if anything new appears on his particular topic.

*Having put a rebuilt on the front I would be in trouble if we did not have an original elsewhere - No 34066 'Spitfire' on the coaling stage at Guildford.*

I think it would be fair to say there cannot be many around with the same degree of knowledge of the area, train workings, operational requirements, associate businesses all trip off the tongue. It was probably no surprise then to learn his passion has resulted in a considerable number of albums of material all related to his one subject. We are grateful for allowing us free access to use what we hope are some of the most interesting images from his collection in this issue and forming the start of what will be several illustrative pieces devoted to the Midhurst lines.

In return Antony has asked for help, obviously any new material would be welcome, but he would also be grateful for any photographs of the following bridges, ideally from road level: Moggs Head or Ramshill Bridge at Petersfield (this was the old A3 to Portsmouth), also Station Road or Bepton Road bridge at Midhurst.

Many readers will be aware that there were a few derailments on the Midhurst lines, probably the best known being that at Cocking Causeway in 1904 and also the culvert washout in 1951 when No 32522 fell into the water beneath. Again Antony would be grateful for any reference to the official reports on these.

Speaking of reports, when an accident or derailment occurred which was not subject to a formal Board of Trade enquiry there would still be an internal report. Does anyone know if any of these (and not just reference Midhurst) survive?

Which leads me on very nicely, so if anyone reading this has their own passion: station, locomotive, line, rolling stock even and you have amassed material, it might be worth a chat to see if we can include something in 'SW'. With what I know is a vast store of knowledge out there it could be even more appears!

Another thought is anniversaries, openings, closures, building, withdrawals even, contributions in this area are also welcome. It need not be a whole article, enough for just one page would suffice.

Finally reference my comments about the future of 'SW' and the likes and dislikes. This has generated an amount of comment. Some have complimentary views, some not so but all appreciated and all constructive. It would be inappropriate to reproduce all views but a sample is shown in 'Rebuilt'.

*Kevin Robertson*

**Front cover -** *Power and majesty at Bournemouth Central. In the minds of many, still one of the best if not the best looking steam machine running in BR days. Arthur King*

**Pages 2/3 -** *One of the final if not the final Royal working for a 'Schools', No 30926 'Repton' waiting departure from Tattenham Corner......*

**Rear cover -** *'Last days at Fullerton, 26 August 1964', passenger services were withdrawn just two weeks later. Terry Tracey*

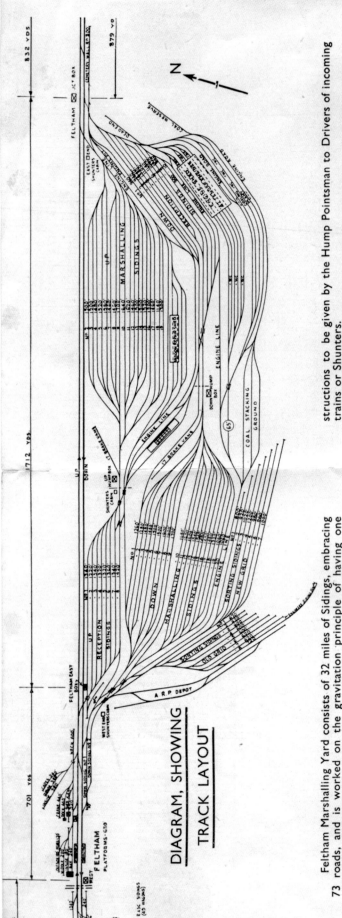

## DIAGRAM, SHOWING TRACK LAYOUT

Feltham Marshalling Yard consists of 32 miles of Sidings, embracing 73 roads, and is worked on the gravitation principle of having one "Hump" in the Down Yard and one "Hump" in the Up Yard.

Down Yard trains are mainly received from other Regions via the following junctions :-

| | | |
|---|---|---|
| Eastern Region | G.C. Section | Via Neasden, Kew and Hounslow, |
| | G.N. Section | Metropolitan Lines, Blackfriars Bridge and Barnes, |
| | G.E. Section | Temple Mills, Willesden, Kew and Hounslow, |
| London Midland Region | N.W Section | Willesden, Kew and Hounslow, |
| | Midland Section | Brent, Kew and Hounslow, |

and from the Southern Region (London East Division) via Clapham Junction.

Up Yard trains are received from the South-West and West of England via Chertsey, and from the Western Region via Reading. Local Suburban Services work into both Yards.

Approximately 68 trains arrive and 73 depart every 24 hours, and additional special trains as required.

There are eight Up Reception Sidings capable of holding trains of 60 wagons each, and there are ten Down Reception Sidings.

From the Reception Sidings wagons are shunted over a hump to a series of tracks on the opposite side which spread out fanwise from the foot of the hump.

The movement of trains towards the humps is controlled by signals which can be operated either from the hump boxes or by Shunter from ground level. These signals work in conjunction with a "Klaxon" horn which is situated half way in the Reception sidings. The sounding of the horn warns the Driver of the Hump shunting engine by a code of hoots as to the position of the signal, whether in the "On," or "Off" In order to assist generally the working of the Reception sidings, a loud-speaker unit is installed in both hump boxes which permits verbal instructions to be given by the Hump Pointsman to Drivers of incoming trains or Shunters.

Moving very steadily the engine pushes the train of wagons to be split up at about 2 m.p.h. up the hump. The Leading Shunter on the hump uncouples the wagons and chalks on the first wagon the number of the road to which it is to run, and this is observed by the Hump Box Pointsman, who sets the road by pressing the buttons so required on his diagrammatic board. As this wagon passes him he observes the number chalked on its rear end, and this tells him which road is required for the next shunt. In fact, after the first wagon has been dealt with the Pointsman does not require to pay any attention to the train which is being shunted, but only to observe the number chalked on each wagon as it passes him and to set the road accordingly as soon as it clears the points. A powerful electric lamp is provided at one corner of the Signal Box so that the numbers in chalk can be seen after dark, its rays being directed to show them up at the most convenient position for observation. In the War years, the numbers had to be announced to the Pointsman over a Loudaphone by a man on the ground, which method is also used during dense fog. The Hump Boxes are electrically controlled and have been designed to suit conditions at Feltham.

The Up hump provides access to 18 Marshalling Sidings from which goods trains depart for other Regions and for local stations to London.

The Down hump leads to 20 Marshalling Sidings from which departure is made for points in West and South-West England, also Suburban stations via Chertsey

The normal average day turnover is 2,750 wagons in and 2,750 wagons out. These figures do not include transfers from Up to Down Yard and vice versa, or internal working. During ideal conditions, some 7,000 wagons have been dealt with in one day during War period.

In the centre between Up and Down Yards are cattle pens for feeding and watering cattle in transit, a Dock for transhipping loads from defective wagons, a large wagon Repair Depot and an Office.

# SOUTHERN FREIGHT CONTRASTS

## Jeremy Clarke

When Robert Urie and Richard Maunsell were both faced with the problem of supplying engines for two particular duties the solutions they came up with, despite appearing quite unalike, had a number of basic similarities.

Both men were required to provide a heavy shunting locomotive and a class specifically for cross-London transfer traffic. They chose to build tank engines for these tasks and both decided to fit eight coupled wheels to the shunters and six to the 'runners', but each in their way reflected the standards adopted in their own railway spheres and experience, which is not to say one result was superior to the other. More significantly perhaps, both used many readily available parts, thus saving cost. For the work they were designed to do, all four products excelled.

Urie's requirement came about directly as a result of the construction of Feltham marshalling yard. This was mainly designed to permit the South Western to take over the sorting of its own London area goods traffic. For many years the North Western had carried out much of this activity on its behalf at Willesden. Feltham also relieved pressure on the already overcrowded facilities at Nine Elms goods depot, where there simply was insufficient room to expand. Concomitant traffic costs were rising, not just through the charges made by the LNWR but also from demurrage on wagons that were held awaiting loading or unloading.

Choosing to build on a greenfield site at Feltham meant direct available access to the yard not only from much of the LSWR network – and away from the busy main line approaching London too - but also to and from yards of railways north of the Thames via the North & South Western Junction Railway at Kew. Cricklewood, Neasden, Willesden and Old Oak Common could all be reached directly via this line, Ferme Park and Stratford also by onward use of the Tottenham & Hampstead Junction Railway. The staging point for such traffic up to this time and indeed for some years beyond, were sidings laid between Brentford and Kew Old Junction where the N&SWJR diverged. These were also used to sort wagons for local South Western destinations from those bound north of the Thames. This was particularly true of longer distance services, for example trains emanating from such places as Southampton, Salisbury and Portsmouth. It was clearly more economical to dispatch as much traffic as possible to Brentford in a single train with one engine to divide it into several lesser ones each individually headed.

A site of some forty acres on the south side of the Windsor line between Feltham Junction and station was purchased in 1911. Another forty acres or so were acquired in 1915. The lineal distance is about 1¼ miles but the yard was not level, the line falling eastwards from the station at 1 in 653. The east end of the yard was thus some ten feet lower than the west end.

Plans had been finalised in 1916. These showed six

*Left* - Part of a BR produced leaflet affording a diagram for and details of Feltham yard,

*Right* - The down marshalling yard hump at Feltham looking east on 2 August 1928. Edward Wallis

*'H16' No 30518 4-6-2T outside the depot at Feltham on 20 September 1958.*

reception roads and seventeen sorting sidings in the down section of the yard and eight reception and sixteen sidings in the up side. Because of the height difference between the yard's west and east ends, the up reception sidings were on a downward gradient of 1 in 5,000 but the down ones rose at 1 in 223. Later augmentation brought the down side yard to ten reception and twenty sorting sidings while the up side saw an increase to nineteen sorting roads though the reception yard was not enlarged. There were also two grids containing between them fifteen sidings where the make-up of trains could be refined. These sidings were at the down end but remote from the main groups. Immediately before the Second World War, forty-five down arrivals and twenty-two down departures were scheduled at the yard daily: in the up direction these were respectively twenty-four and forty-five. The variation is a reflection particularly of the number of railways/yards serviced off the Southern as well as transfer traffic to and from Nine Elms.

Each section of the yard worked on the 'Hump' principle, a novel concept in this country at the time. The humps were 7'3" above ambient ground level, the up one with a level section 40' long on the top being approached on a gradient of 1 in 40 with a following downgrade starting at 1 in 50 for 170' and then at 1 in 150 for a further 580'. The down hump gradients were 1 in 60 up and 1 in 50 down for 170' easing to 1 in 150 for another 575'. Large-scale track-

circuiting was installed as well as hydraulically-operated wagon retarders controlled, together with the pointwork, from a box beside each hump. The first part of Feltham yard, a section of nine down sidings, opened days before Christmas 1917 but it was another four years before the whole became fully operational.

A large locomotive depot with a 'through' shed of six roads was set out at the up end of the yard complex. It opened in 1922 and at its height had an allocation of around eighty engines, mainly but not exclusively freight types. (Five 0-4-4T of classes M7 and T1 were on the books in January 1947 as well as several examples of the mixed traffic K10 and L11 4-4-0s.) The depot at Strawberry Hill was closed in 1923 as a result of Feltham's commissioning. This shed had been responsible for working local freight services as well as pre-electrification suburban passenger trains. It retained responsibility for some of the outer-suburban passenger work and sourced engines for the smaller depots at Chertsey and Ascot. A relatively new shed, dating from 1897, it had been enlarged as early as 1906. The site became an EMU depot following the rundown in 1923: it is still in operation.

For use at Feltham, Robert Urie was required to provide engines powerful enough to shunt substantial trains up and over the humps and for this he turned out a new design. But for transfer traffic Urie took his S15 class 4-6-0

*Southern Railway publicity department image of 'H15' 4-6-0 No 478 leaving Feltham Yard on 9 July 1942. The headcode is a Nine Elms to Southampton Docks working via Brentford, Chertsey and Woking. No 92 was a Nine Elms duty.*

as the basis of the new engine. The S15-pattern frames were lengthened and supported by a trailing truck to accommodate a bunker holding 3½ tons of coal. Side tanks had a capacity of 2000 gallons of water. The S15-type 21"x28" cylinders and 5'7" coupled wheels were also used, though the parallel boiler was of slightly smaller dimensions than that of the S15. Pressed at 180psi, it offered 1406 sq ft of heating surface of which 139 sq ft was in the firebox, while Urie's superheater had an area of 231 sq ft. Grate area was 27 sq ft. Tractive effort at 85%BP was calculated at 28,200lbs, the same as the S15. The overall design was both aesthetically and operationally successful. The engines turned the scales at 96t 8cwt in working order.

All five of the class, designated H16 and numbered 516-20, were built at Eastleigh in 1921 and later were re-equipped with a Maunsell superheater. Although of smaller heating surface than Urie's, it was easier to remove when maintenance was needed. Its installation was made obvious by the two snifting valves high up on the sides of the smokebox, though these were later found to be of little merit and were removed.

Like all the others specified by Urie, this engine

was worked out in detail at Eastleigh by Thomas 'Jock' Finlayson. He had served his apprenticeship with Neilson, Reid in Glasgow and later rose to be a leading draughtsman at North British. It is very likely their paths had crossed professionally before Urie recruited him from there in 1913 to be his Chief Draughtsman. Finlayson had most definite ideas about the superiority of Eastleigh, contending among other things that the Urie N15s were in no way inferior to the Maunsell 'King Arthurs' and to say so showed Ashford's propaganda had successfully – and unjustly! - had a malign influence on opinion. His attitude later brought him into muted conflict with the widely experienced James Clayton, who twice held a similar position at Ashford. In 1919 Clayton, who had returned to Ashford in 1914 after an absence of eleven years, became Maunsell's personal assistant and later his deputy, a post he retained after Grouping.

Finlayson also worked out the design of the shunting locomotive, the G16 4-8-0T, the only class built by the South Western with eight coupled wheels. Four engines were introduced in 1921 numbered 492-5 and despite being 'new' some readily available items went into them. Among

*One of the eight members of the 'Z' class, intended for heavy shunting. Is that a shunter's truck immediately behind the engine?*

these were 5'1" driving wheels, an LSWR standard size for years, and N15-type 22"x28" cylinders. The same boiler as on the H16 also featured. Urie fitted superheaters to these engines as well, because the original intention at the planning stage had been to make use of them if necessary on short trip workings as well as shunting. In the event this did not happen as often as envisaged, though such work became more frequent post-war. Superheaters were found, in general, to be of little, if any, use in shunting work, the primary function of the class, though Maunsell actually installed his own pattern in the boilers when the original Urie type were life expired.

The 3½ ton capacity bunker matched that of the H16 as did the 2000-gallon water capacity, though the tanks themselves differed in shape. To assist lookout when climbing the hump, the forward part of the tank was sloped sharply downward. To compensate for this, the rear part rose much higher up the cab front than was the case with the H16, perversely making the cab 'lights' smaller. And because of the 4-8-0 wheel arrangement, the ashpan sat above the driving wheel axles rather than between them as with the H16. Thus the firebox was not quite as deep. In working order these locos weighed 95t 2cwt. Tractive effort at 85%BP was 33,940lbs: in those terms these were by some way the most powerful engines to be built by the LSWR.

The four spent their entire careers based at Feltham other than a short period allocated to Strawberry Hill before the depot was ready. No 492 was withdrawn in 1959 and the other three had gone by the end of 1962.

The big Pacific tanks, while mainly employed on the cross-London work for which they were designed, ranged a little more widely. Indicative of that perhaps is that under the Southern regime they were turned out in passenger green livery, hence the 'Green Tanks' colloquial name bestowed by enginemen. Ironically however, they very rarely featured on passenger workings but could be regularly seen on trains of empty stock into and out of Waterloo. This particularly applied to destinations beyond Clapham Junction, such places as Chertsey, or Oatlands Sidings between Walton-on-Thames and Weybridge. As with the G16, these five spent almost all their working lives based at Feltham and all five remained in service until 1962. No engine of either class has been preserved.

When Richard Maunsell came upon the same problem as Urie faced almost a decade before, the Southern was fully committed to large scale electrification with Herbert Walker already contemplating extending the third rail to the coast. Thus funds for steam locomotive development and construction were seriously limited. But with freight trains becoming longer and heavier the need for

*A member of the 'W' class on the 'Ludgate' line approaching Factory Junction with what is probably a cross-London freight off the West London Extension. Headcode, no 9, as applied here is 'London and Hither Green Sidings, hence the destination at least is obvious. The signalling is still semaphore - colour-lights came in at this location in 1959. Note too the early BR livery rolling stock in the sidings.*

more powerful shunting engines than the (generally) small and often superannuated machines used for such work, had been identified.

It ought to be pointed out that Maunsell was first and foremost a very fine administrator with a locomotive engineering background and, as in the case of the relationship between Urie and Finlayson at Eastleigh, he delegated much of the work to his Chief Draughtsman, William Hooley. Like most men in a post of that title, Hooley lived in the background, in the shadow of his chief who inevitably took the plaudits for a successful design as well as the brickbats for one that did not come up to scratch. Hooley had joined the South Eastern & Chatham Railway in January 1913, right at the end of Wainwright's tenure. Like Finlayson, he had come from a private manufacturing base, in this case in his native Manchester. His apprenticeship had been served with Beyer Peacock – where, incidentally, James Clayton also learned his trade as an apprentice between 1893 and 1899 - and after that he went to work for Nasmyth Wilson until, at age twenty-five, coming south to Ashford.

In a move Finlayson was offered but refused, preferring to stay on and continue to wield some influence at Eastleigh, Hooley became the Southern Railway's Leading Locomotive Draughtsman in 1924 following the relocation of the drawing office to Waterloo. Before then, however, he had been responsible for much of the basic design work for Maunsell at Ashford. For example, very probably at Clayton's direction, Hooley laid out the very successful N class Mogul of 1917, a class extensively multiplied on the Southern to eighty units and eventually appearing all over the system. That same year another Hooley engine, the very handsome K class 2-6-4 tank appeared. In this case the drawing that formed the basis of this design and indeed for the whole of Maunsell's mogul family, had been set out by Clayton soon after his arrival back at Ashford in 1914. Herbert Holcroft, who had come that year from the very

forward-looking Swindon drawing office at Maunsell's behest, considered it smacked far too much of the Midland. As Clayton had filled the post of Chief Assistant at the Derby drawing office from 1907 that is, perhaps, not so surprising. It should he noted however that long travel valves were shown, though which of Holcroft or Maunsell instigated this, one cannot know now. Certainly Holcroft, with his Swindon experience, must have influenced matters in this respect.

History has dealt unkindly with the K, mainly because of the involvement of No. 800, *River Cray*, in the Sevenoaks disaster of August 1927 when the engine derailed at speed and not, within the class, for the first time. The ex-South Eastern main line was then still largely ballasted with Dungeness shingle bound with ash, a quite unsuitable base for the faster and heavier trains now regularly in use. The line in general had taken a terrible pounding during the years of the First World War and the maintenance arrears that resulted from that very demanding period had not been made up to any great extent. On top of that, the summer of 1927 had been unseasonably wet.

Following subsequent tests, the engines were deemed to be 'track-sensitive', though Brighton-line men, well used to handling large tank engines on somewhat better ballasted, if still rather indifferent, track, had not made any formal complaint. They did, however, comment on the liveliness of the riding – 'prance and dance' as one retired engineman neighbour who fired them once described it to me. Hooley's work, it seems, was condemned in this case by circumstances largely beyond his control. Maunsell, of course, took the blame for the problem and acceded to Walker's suggestion that they be converted to tender engines. The 'U' class, another Hooley design based on the 1914 drawing, but as a tender engine version, and with production poised to get under way at the time, absorbed the rebuilt 'Rivers'. But one of the 'K' class, no 890, *River Frome*, had been built as a three-cylinder machine with

Holcroft conjugated gear for the middle valve and designated K1 when coming into service in 1925. (This engine eventually formed the prototype for the U1 Moguls.)

Holcroft's system provided more accurate and constant valve events than the better known Gresley variety, because the drive to the front of the centre valve was taken directly from the head of the combination lever rather than extension of the outside valve spindle. Thus Holcroft's avoided any change in the valve events caused by those spindles as they heated up with use and expanded. But to activate the middle valve in this way the drive rod had to be taken past the outer valve chest which, for this reason, was set well in from the longitudinal line of the cylinder itself. Only one other Southern engine had this gear fitted, the prototype N1 class Mogul no. 822 of 1923. But the gear did not survive on either of these two locos, the centre valve later being fitted with Walschaerts gear. Apart from the production N1 and U1, the 'Schools' were the only other 3-

cylinder engines of the Maunsell years that had independent Walschaerts gear from the first. But Maunsell chose to work the three N1-type 16"x28" cylinders into both his new classes.

The shunting engine came first. The eight locomotives in the class, numbered 950-7, were built at Brighton in 1929. Maunsell had briefly considered adding to the G16s with some modifications but decided against it. The Z class was the only Maunsell eight-coupled engine to get beyond the drawing board, Hooley having previously laid out two unbuilt 2-8-0T designs in 1919 for the SECR but rejected by the Civil Engineer on the grounds of weight. Oddly enough Holcroft conjugated valve gear was planned for this new shunting engine but civil engineering objections to the excessive distance between the front buffer beam and the leading wheels prevented it. (Why rejection for that particular reason is not clear.)

Maunsell then considered providing a trailing pony

*'H16' No 30517 at Thorpe Crossing, between Egham and Staines, taken from the footbridge across the line. 7 May 1950.*

truck but discarded the idea because of the reduction in adhesion weight that would result. Thus the 0-8-0T came into being with an overhang at each end of all but 11'. However, while Walschaerts gear drove the outside valves, a form of Marshall gear was fitted to work the inside valve, its extra eccentric providing lap and lead movement. The inside cylinder drove the second axle and was angled at 1 in 8 to clear the leading axle.

Maunsell took other factors into account, not least that some of the Southern's marshalling yards were in built-up areas, Norwood and Hither Green for example. He could not quieten the clashing of wagon buffers but wanted to avoid any unnecessary noise from the locomotive. The three-cylinder layout was used because it not only produced a more even torque than two cylinders but also thus lessened the likelihood of slipping and the resulting violent exhaust as well as providing six softer beats per revolution.

The boiler, pressed at 180psi, was a Brighton standard of good capacity - 1,279 sq ft - of which the firebox contributed 106 sq ft - but Maunsell allied it to a relatively small grate with an area of only 18.6 sq ft. The ratios in these dimensions, Maunsell believed, would cause the fire to die down quickly after shunting. Thus it would restrict unnecessary blowing-off through the safety valves, something particularly to be avoided during the inevitable periods of inactivity inherent in shunting. On the other hand

it was deemed the residual heat stored in the boiler, if boosted by a few shovelsful of fresh coal on to the fire, would make the engine ready for immediate use when required.

No superheater was fitted, Maunsell reasoning it would be superfluous simply because, in the relatively short time it took to shunt a train, superheating to any meaningful degree would not occur. Unlike Urie's shunters, there was never any intention of using the 'Z' class for trip work which handicapped them somewhat on particular duties in their final days.

The bunker held three tons of coal but the tanks, the forward end sloping for good lookout as in the 'G16', had a capacity of only 1500 gallons. Here again is an indication of the planned restriction of use: water was always available in a goods yard. Only the driving wheels at 4'8" diameter were non-standard. Why Maunsell chose this odd size is a mystery as Brighton had turned out innumerable engines with 4'6" wheels. Using that size could have made a marginal reduction possible in the fixed wheelbase of 17'6" as well as providing a slight increase in the tractive effort at 85%BP of 29,375lbs. The all-up weight of the engines in working order was given as 71t 12cwt.

Knowing how tortuous goods yard sidings could be, Maunsell provided the leading and trailing axles with a degree of side-play that enabled the loco to negotiate curves

*An 'H16' at Guildford was slightly unusual, although here No 30518 is recorded having arrived with a freight from Woking, 23 November 1957. the headcode is No 21, 'W'loo/Nine Elms-Portsmouth via Woking and Guildford'. The implication here is that this came down the main line rather than via Feltham and Staines although the engine displays a Feltham duty number. (Going via Feltham, at least as far as Woking, would require code 16.)*     *David Fereday-Glenn*

down to 4½ chains radius at dead slow speed. Actually getting round such a tight curvature could only be achieved if there was sufficient clearance for the long overhangs. The class was fitted with vacuum brakes and steam heating apparatus. The brakes allowed fitted freight traffic to be worked but on the face of it, the provision of steam heating appears to have been wholly unnecessary. Perhaps it was believed the engines would thus be capable of heating empty stock coming into service.

These locos proved to be very efficient – and quiet! – shunters though their numbers were never increased. Another batch of ten was scheduled for construction at Eastleigh in 1931 but the poor economic situation caused cancellation. By the time more shunting engines were needed, diesel-electrics had already proved their worth on the LMS and GWR. Ashford built three 0-6-0 diesel shunters in 1937 with English Electric equipment, forerunners of a host that became classes 08 and 09 in BR

days. Paradoxically, the three were all allocated new to Norwood Junction, which never had a member of the Z class on its books. (It is believed the numbers of these three diesels were to have followed those of the Z class, i.e. 958-60, but in the event they became prosaically 1, 2 and 3, 15201-3 in BR days.)

Members of the Z class put in a short and rather unsuccessful appearance in early 1951 on the Fawley branch. The Anglo-Gulf West Indies Petroleum Company promoted this under a Light Railway Order to serve their refineries at Fawley, the LSWR to work the line. That company took it over in July 1922 though construction did not start until after Grouping. It opened from a junction at Totton on 20th July 1925. Passenger services were never particularly heavy though they survived until February 1966. On the other hand freight, and petroleum products in particular, grew to the extent that additional sidings and passing loops continued to be added over the years. Such traffic is still carried though in lesser quantities.

Towards the end of their service three of the Z class, Nos. 950/5/6, were shedded at Exmouth Junction for banking and piloting work on the 1 in 37 incline between St David's and Central. In some respects this posting should have played to their strengths as they were designed for a short, sharp burst of energy rather than a long drawn out one. They were thus fairly successful though some reports suggest very skilled handling and firing were required if they were not to become short of breath before Central was reached, especially if the train were particularly heavy. Taken together with their use at Fawley here was evidence of the limits of the boiler proportions for anything other than the locos' designed purpose.

Other Z class engines finished their days at Ashford and Salisbury, though no. 953 found itself for a time at Templecombe. As well as its shunting duties, this saw it getting involved in the transfer of trains between the Southern station and Templecombe No 2 Junction on the Somerset & Dorset line. All eight had gone by the end of 1962.

The inter-regional freight traffic that had been a feature of cross-London workings from very early on in railway history had been largely in the hands of relatively small goods locomotives until the LSWR H16 put in its appearance. By 1931 the Southern's widespread electrification of the suburban area had brought significantly faster and more frequent passenger services. This situation highlighted the need for an engine capable of working longer and heavier transfer freight trains than had been customary and running them at a generally higher speed too. Not only would such trains be less costly to work than two or three lighter ones but they would make best use of the limited paths available.

The main cross-London routes abounded in curves and gradients which made not just power but also efficient braking a necessity for hauling loose-coupled goods trains. With that in mind, Maunsell set out the specification for the drawing office for a class to meet these needs. As before, costs would be kept to a minimum by making use of standard parts so far as was possible. The result was the W class 2-6-4T, five engines, Nos. 1911-5, being turned out by Eastleigh in 1932. Other than the 'Z' class with its restricted traffic application and the 'E1R' rebuilds, this was the first tank engine produced by Maunsell since the fateful Sevenoaks disaster of 1927. Even that provided a side benefit for the cabs and water tanks removed from the converted 'Rivers' were reused on the new engines with slight modification, a near copy of the configuration on the single member of class K', for this new class.

The W was effectively a tank locomotive version of the N1 class of 1922, having the same three cylinders but with an extra ½" on the diameter at 16½"x28". The inside cylinder was worked by a modified form of Holcroft's conjugated gear. In this case however the drive was made to the rear of the valve spindle by cross rods from the tops of the outside combination levers. The boiler came straight off the N design. Pressed at 200psi it offered 1,526 sq ft of heating surface of which the firebox contributed 135 sq ft, the grate area being 25 sq ft. A Maunsell superheater of 285 sq ft was fitted. Similarly, N-type driving wheels of 5'6" were provided though the coupled wheelbase was six inches shorter, the rear drivers being that much closer to the centre pair. At 85%BP the tractive effort was calculated as 29,452lbs. With the bunker holding 3½ tons of coal and the tanks 2000 gallons the all-up weight of this very handsome machine was 90t 14cwt. In line with the N1 the maximum width of the engine was 8' 6½" giving it good route availability.

Bogies recovered from the 'River's were also used but fitted with brakes, steam-operated as were those on the driving wheels which were given a high brake force.

The leading pony truck came from remnants of stock acquired from Woolwich which, to maintain a degree of employment there after the First World War, had produced, with Government funding, parts for one hundred N class 2-6-0s. Vacuum brakes and steam-heat equipment were provided: the former was obviously needed to work fully or partially fitted freights. The Chief Engineer, George Ellson, still haunted by his memories of Sevenoaks, which happened not long after he had succeeded Alfred Szlumper as Chief Engineer, had a horror of a heavy locomotive with a leading pony truck working fast traffic. He therefore forbade the use of the W class on passenger trains even though that was not the intention. Steam-heating therefore was only for the benefit of ripening bananas or warming empty coaching stock. Ellson, for the same reason, caused the plans for Maunsell's heavy 2-6-2 mixed-traffic loco of 1934 to be dumped in the bin and another batch of S15 engines turned out of Eastleigh in 1936 instead, (nos. 838-47). These ten had slight Maunsell-inspired modifications.

Despite Ellson's embargo the Ws worked empty stock quite frequently, particularly post-WW2 and Bulleid actually tried out No. 1918 on passenger trains on the lines to Ashford from Tonbridge and Maidstone. The object was to compare performance against the LMS Fairburn 4MT class 2-6-4T, two of which, Nos 41298 and 41299, were involved to test their suitability for Southern metals. The result, surprisingly, was not very successful though it has to be pointed out the Ws were rated in a pure freight classification – '6' - and not in a mixed-traffic one. Fairburns were later turned out by Brighton Works for service on the Southern Region, forty-one being constructed in two lots in 1950/1. All were later dispatched to their spiritual home on the London Midland which ceded 'Standard' class 4MT 2-6-4Ts in their place, many of which had been constructed at Brighton alongside their LMS antecedents.

The W class could not, however, be surpassed on the work for which it had been designed. Ashford turned out ten more in 1935/6, nos. 1916-25. These engines had left-

*Opposite page* - In order to improve efficiency in night shunting (remember at the time the railways were running, receiving, shunting, marshalling, and despatching freight at the main yards 24hrs a day), some lighting trials were carried out at the yards at both Feltham and Hither Green in 1947. Top left is the lighting assembly on the ground at Feltham and with three brake vans in the background.

*Bottom left* is the temporary lighting tower at the same location.

*Opposite page, bottom right* - Obviously the trials were satisfactory as lighting towers were provided.

*This page* - Three views of how night might be turned into day at Hither Green, probably around the same time. A little different to just a few short years before traffic density was even heavier and all that was available to the men was an oil hand-lamp.

*Collection Steve Godden*

*A final view of an illuminated Hither Green included as it shows the top of what is believed to be one of the SR diesel shunters beneath.*

hand drive as opposed to the right-hand drive of the first five. They also had steam sanding, the earlier batch's gravity sanding being changed to conform in the late-1950s.

For much of their lives the engines were divided among just three depots, Stewarts Lane, Norwood Junction and Hither Green. The latter two sheds were, of course, located cheek-by-jowl with the major London marshalling yards of the Southern's Central and Eastern Divisions respectively. Only toward the very end of their existence did any move further afield. Nos. 1912/4/24 were at Feltham in 1963 to take over the duties of withdrawn H16s and four others appeared at Exmouth Junction for banking duties following withdrawal of the Z class engines. No. 1923 was the first withdrawal of the class, in February 1963, and all had gone by the following year, nos. 1912/4 from the earlier batch and then at Feltham being the last, in August. As a matter of interest, representatives of both the H16 and W classes followed the Zs to Fawley in 1960 and 1961, Nos. 517 and 1911 among them. They were presumably more successful than the Z simply because they were doing the sort of heavy freight transfer work for which they had been designed.

By their very nature freight engines never had a following like that drawn by the glamorous passenger classes. But if the Southern was alone in making more of its money from passengers than freight, the other three pre-Nationalisation companies would certainly rate very highly the value of these SR freight classes. While the Southern and its constituents never worked the great plodding cavalcades so common elsewhere, the locomotives both Urie and Maunsell brought to solve their companies' particular traffic needs were among the best.

Bibliography

Richard Maunsell, An Engineering Biography, J E Chacksfield, The Oakwood Press, 1998,
History of the Southern Railway, C F Dendy Marshall, rev. R W Kidner, Ian Allan Ltd., 1963.
Sir Herbert Walker's Southern Railway, C F Klapper, Ian Allan Ltd., 1973.
The South Western Railway, C Hamilton Ellis, George Allen and Unwin, 1956.
Locomotives Illustrated, nos 18 and 105, Maunsell/Southern Moguls, Ian Allan Ltd., May 1979 and January 1996.
Locomotives Illustrated, no 41, LSWR/SR 'H15' and 'S15' 4-6-0s, Ian Allan Ltd., March 1985.
Article 'The James Clayton Influence' by Philip Atkins, 'Railways South East', Ed. David Jenkinson, vol. 1 no 3.
Articles by the author in 'Steam World', issues 248, 249, 253, (Feb, March, July 2008), Steam World Publishing.
Various editions of 'ABC of Southern Locomotives', Ian Allan Ltd, including Combined volumes.

References to the Fawley branch are taken particularly from a recent and really splendid publication, 'Southern Rails Around Southampton' by Ian Drummond, Holne Publishing, 2011.

*Reported as being a test-train at Frost lane level crossing on the Fawley branch - date unknown. This would have been to assess the suitability of the class for hauling heavy oil tank car trains from Fawley. J Courtenay-Hayden*

*Feltham yard with 'S15' No 30499 leaving to head west - notwithstanding the headcode: No 6 which covers workings between Feltham and Willesden via Kew East Junction. (Members of the 'S15' class having a bogie tender were generally barred from the Brighton main line.) Alongside is 350hp diesel shunter No 13042, which in 1958 at least was based at Feltham. It is odd that the two trains on this page both display the same headcode, No 6. The H16 carries it for 'Eastleigh/Southampton and Fawley', the S15 'W'loo/Nine Elms-Reading via Twickenham'. It seems likely we have here Eastleigh and Nine Elms duties respectively.*

# EASTLEIGH 1941

## Images from the Curl Collection at the National Railway Museum

Amidst the dark days of WW2 a new creation takes shape at Eastleigh. I recall seeing some of these views in 'Bulleid: Last Giant of Steam', one of the first railway books I ever read. The story and imagery has remained with me for - shall we be polite and just say a few years - and it was thus both a privilege and an opportunity to locate some of the views again (plus a few others) whilst investigating the Curl collection in late 2013.

We can only wonder what might have been going through the minds of those working on bringing the first of these monsters to life. Certainly nothing like it had been seen anywhere before whilst it was also by far the largest steam design ever to have been built at Eastleigh - a record that will never now be surpassed.

Was Bulleid's creation really a mixed-traffic design, or was he and the board of the Southern conveniently ignoring the dire position the country was then in? Certainly there were those amongst the workforce then at Eastleigh who were seriously concerned over the construction of what they saw as one man's dream, considering at the time they would be better placed producing machines more obviously suited to the war effort.

The fact the men were placated is perhaps in part due to the charisma of the designer, whilst later there was much publicity given to the engines hauling freight workings and so justifying the criteria of a 'mixed-traffic' design, a designation that appears to have been conveniently dropped in later years.

Above, what would be No 21C1 later 'Channel Packet' sits in the erecting shop in late 1940. Notice the steps at the front seemingly lettered with the initials 'M-N' but more likely the coincidental initials of the gang foreman. The small splashers to the driving wheels may be noted.

Right - Wheeling in progress and complete.

*Left - Front bogie and pony truck have been removed although the cab sides may be seen fitted plus various items of pipework. In the foreground are those additional rods forged and machined ready for other members of the class?*

*Bottom - From the opposite side, clacks added, also coupling / connecting rods.*

EASTLEIGH 1941

**Above -** *Slightly back in time but of interest as this also shows the regulator handle which could be operated from either side of the footplate.*

**Right -** *Minus cab, but ready for valve setting.*

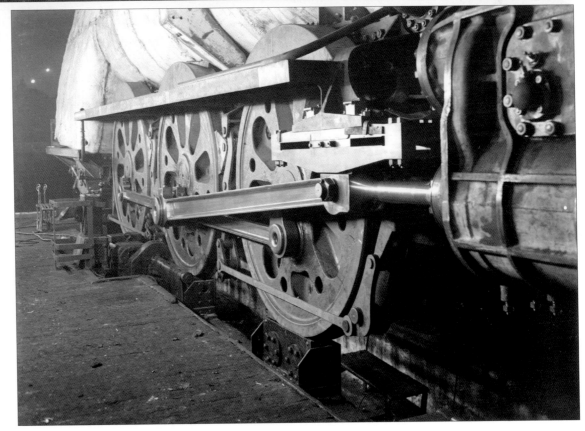

*Opposite top -*
*Valve setting, note too what appears to be asbestos blanket insulation to the boiler and firebox.*

*Opposite bottom -*
*Piles of main frames cut and ready for use.*

***This page top, left and right -*** *Front end and tender from 21C7 which was completed at Eastleigh and entered traffic in June 1942.*

***Right -*** *Multiple jet blast pipe and white-painted smokebox interior.*

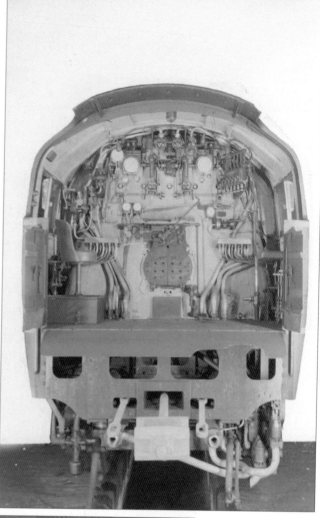

*Above left and right -* Variations in Bulleid cab design. Notice the seat, background to the gauge glasses and cocks on the steam manifold.

*Left -* Patterns / samples for two nameplate centres. The reference to 'Royal Mail' is slightly puzzling as the flag design was different.

# SUSSEX RAILTOUR: 24 June 1962

## Robert Wigley

At the risk of over-using the phrase 'A Grand Day-Out', the Locomotive Club of Great Britain 'Sussex Railtour' of 24 June 1962 was one on which the gods of sunshine certainly shone. Involved was slightly over 233 miles of travel with five different

2nd - SPECIAL EXCURSION
The Locomotive Club of Great Britain
"THE SUSSEX COAST LIMITED"
(C.M. 8549) Sunday 24th JUNE, 1962.
WATERLOO-GUILDFORD-HORSHAM-
MIDHURST-BOGNOR REGIS-
HAYWARDS HEATH-EASTBOURNE-
HEATHFIELD-LONDON BRIDGE-
(S)                               (S)
FOR CONDITIONS SEE OVER
0109     0109

4

5

steam engines, either singly or in multiple whilst behind throughout was seven-coach passenger set No 237.

Leaving Waterloo exactly at the booked departure time of 9.42 am., 'T9' No 120 took the line west and then south west through Clapham Junction, Surbiton and Effingham Junction to arrive at Guildford (1) at 10.37 am where the engine was booked to take water. Twelve minutes later No 120 was on the move again travelling south before turning off the main line at Peasmarsh Junction and shortly afterwards making a photo-stop at Cranleigh (2). After this it was non-stop to Horsham where ten minutes had been allowed to change engines, although in the event a two minute early arrival still result in a two minute late departure.

Two former LBSCR 0-6-2Ts now took charge, E4 No 32503 and E6 No 32417 on the route south past Itchingfield Junction, Pulborough, Hardham Junction, Selham (3-photo stop) and Midhurst (4) where there was an on-time arrival at 12.52 pm. Here the engines would run-round with the scheduled departure of 1.07 pm. For

reasons that are not stated, departure was not until 1.17 pm retracing the same path as far as Pulborough where there was another engine change.

Now it was the turn of 'K' class 2-6-0 No 32353 (5) to head south and then west through Arundel and Barnham to the next destination point of Bognor Regis. Here a 36 minute layover had been arranged for the engine to be turned although a late arrival meant the special was still one minute late against the scheduled departure time of 2 55 pm.

No 32353 rejoined the main line this time turning east and then joined the main Brighton line south of Preston Park to reach Haywards Heath. The 'T9' joined the train again here resulting in another reversal of direction south to Keymer Junction (for the second time in less than 30 minutes) and then running via Lewes, Southeram Junction and Polegate to the final south coast destination at Eastbourne 6 & 7).

Just over one hour was allowed at the Sussex

terminus where No 120 was turned and made ready for departure, 'M7' No 30055 also being coupled ahead (8).

Departure from Eastbourne was via Polegate, Hailsham (six minute stop) to Horam (four minute stop), and then through Heathfield and Mayfield to arrive at Rotherfield four minutes behind schedule at 7.01 pm (9). Here the 'M7' was detached (10), No 120 continuing alone via Redgate Mill Junction, Eridge, Ashurst Junction, East Grinstead, Crowhurst North Junction, Oxted (a final nine minute stop) and thence via South Croydon, Windmill

Bridge Junction, Norwood Junction, Bricklayers Arms Junction, to finally arrive at London Bridge (Low Level) at 8 54 p.m, 13 minutes late, although much of the delay on the final stage was down to signals Selsdon and East Croydon.

Of the locos used, both Nos 32353 and No 32417 lasted a further six months being withdrawn at the end of 1962, No 32503 lasted slightly longer and was withdrawn on 30 April 1963. 'M7' No 30055 was withdrawn on 30 September 1963. 'T9' No 120 is of course preserved.

8

Locations -

1       Guildford
2       Cranleigh
3       Selham
4       Midhurst
5       Pulborough
6       Eastbourne
7       Eastbourne
8       Eastbourne
9       Rotherfield
10      Rotherfield

(Another unrelated special involving a
Southern engine was run on the same day
organised by the 'Home Counties Railway
Club'. This took No 30850 'Lord Nelson'
on a return trip between Paddington and
Swindon.)

# BY LSWR TO MIDHURST

Antony Hemens is a man with a passion. A passion that is for all to do with the railway at and leading to Midhurst. Having had the pleasure of meeting him, it was a revelation to discover he had amassed literally hundreds of images of the three lines to and from the West Sussex town. Antony has kindly allowed us free rein of the collection from which we have selected this first batch out of the literally hundreds available. Here then is a selection of Petersfield and the LSWR line to Midhurst. Captions by Antony Hemens with all views from his own collection (original annotation included where known.) Further pictorial forays covering the lines from Chichester and Pulborough will appear later.

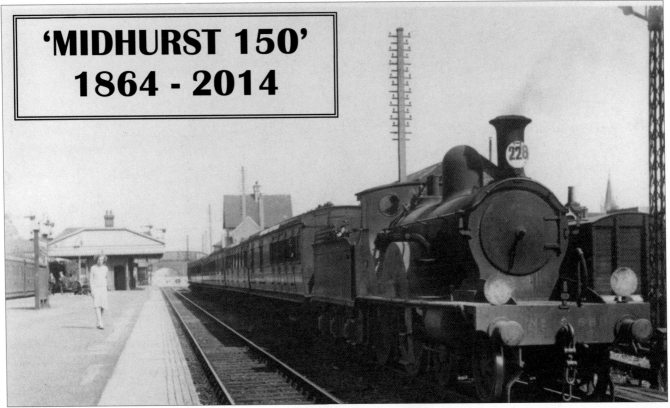

## 'MIDHURST 150' 1864 - 2014

*Above* - LSWR 'X2' 4-4-0 N0 588 pauses at Petersfield with a down Portsmouth Town train. Duty No 228 was a weekday turn from Guildford. The carriage roof boards will be noted as will the choice of couplings available on the drawhook.

*Right -* The (standard) informative nameboard of the period. Depicted here - and also in the view above - is the future Mrs Henry Casserley. In the background another locomotive, (700 class 0-6-0 No 350) is shunting in the yard. The up platform also served as an island at this time. Both images were taken on 30 August 1930.

H C Casserley

*Opposite top* - *From the north end of the Down mainline platform at Petersfield with road traffic in the foreground. (The level crossing is still a major delay to traffic in the 21st century.) At the end of the platform is the starting signal, levers 40/19A/20, controlling Up direction movements from the Down platform. Beyond in the branch platform is the Midhurst branch push-pull set formed of two LSWR non-corridor vehicles running as set No 653. On the opposite side of the line is Petersfield signal box (at various times referred to as Petersfield Junction). At the time it contained a 53 lever frame but this was reduced to just 7 when a mini-panel was installed to control what were by then lifting barriers in 1974. There had originally been a second smaller signal box on the south end of the station controlling access to the numerous sidings in the goods yard on both sides of the main line (see 'SW No 4).*

*Above* - *'M7' No 30109 with a single pull-push coach at Rogate, forming the 12.33 pm Pulborough to Petersfield service sometime in 1954. Whilst some passengers are intent on joining, the revenue accrued from the train would be unlikely to cover operating costs, a feature sadly typical of numerous branch lines at the time.*

*Opposite bottom* - *The divergence of the Midhurst line from the 'Portsmouth direct' was by the overbridge seen in the view above, after which the now single track branch began a curve eastwards. The train seen has just crossed over Howard's farm bridge, the service being the 10.40 am all stations service to Midhurst and Pulborough. 4 February 1955.*

*Right* - *Long time Ganger, Chris Till, at Elsted setting off on his daily inspection of the permanent way and fencing. In the foreground is the ground signal allowing access from the siding on to the running line. Beyond is the loading gauge and goods shed with the passenger platform also visible. There never was a signal box at Elsted station.*

35

*Opposite - In the early years of British Railways, former LBSCR passenger tank engines could be found alternating with LSWR types on 'The Middy' service. Built in the final decade of the Victorian age, Billinton 'D3' 0-4-4T No 32364 of Horsham depot, bustles along the branch with the 10.37 am Petersfield to Midhurst and Pulborough not far out of Elsted.*

*This page top - The first line to reach Midhurst was that from Petersfield, projected by the independent Petersfield Railway Company although absorbed into the LSWR even before opening. Formal opening came on 1 September 1864. To service what was then a terminus, a single road brick built engine shed was provided. This survived the rationalisation of facilities at Midhurst under the Southern Railway in 1925 and was still in use for locomotive purposes until 1937. It is seen here soon*

*after with sections of the roof and the doors already removed. Parts of the shed were still standing in 1955. Just to the north-east of the shed had been a brickworks 'Midhurst Whites', producing sand/ lime bricks. This was serviced by a private siding controlled by a ground frame. The brickworks also had three unconnected 2' 6" railways. The last of these survived until 1976, at the time the final narrow gauge industrial line in Sussex.*

*This page bottom - 'M7' 0-4-4T No 54 passing the now closed LSWR passenger station with a two-coach working. The train has just crossed Bepton Road bridge, the official dividing point between the LSWR and LBSCR systems at Midhurst. As built Bepton Road bridge was not strong enough to support locomotives and whilst a connecting line ran across it joining the two railways, any interchange of traffic involved fly shunting. Passengers had to walk between the two stations. This situation persisted until the absorption of the LSWR and LBSCR by the Southern Railway after which the bridge was strengthened to take locomotives and all trains could use the LBSCR facilities so allowing the LSWR station to close. 26 September 1937.*

*Above* - Looking into Stent's yard at Midhurst. Isidor Livingstone Stent operated a coal business at Midhurst in the 1930s. Some idea of the reliance placed upon coal at the time may be gauged from his use of nine lorries and four horse-drawn carts to supply the town which then had a population of under 2,000, although he would also venture to the surrounding villages but not beyond the next railway station. He ran at least one double Sentinel steam wagon which was supplied new. His fleet also included at least three five-and-seven planks railway vehicles. In addition to his coal business, Mr Stent operated a builders merchants'. He had a second business operating under the name of Farley & Son, also trading in coal but with the addition of corn, cake seed and manure. To complete his portfiolio, he was the cartage contractor and agent for the LSWR in the town.

*Opposite bottom* - Nyewood brickworks Garrett steam lorry in Midhurst LSWR yard next to a 5-plank 'Stent' wagon. (Nyewood brickworks had a private siding a quarter of a mile west of Rogate station.) The Nyewood lorry was often hired by Midhurst Whites to move coal from the LBSCR goods yard to their own works. This was cheaper than requesting the Southern Railway to deliver direct to the LSWR site.

*This page, top and centre* - The road fleet of Messrs I Stent, note the private owner wagons in the background to the top view. An 'AA' badge may be noted above the registration number in the centre view.

*This page, bottom* - Persons unknown at Midhurst LSWR including a very stern looking gentleman. The LSWR goods shed is in the background and also two private owner wagons. One is Wm Cory & Co., the second likely to be either Baldwin or Botrill. Behind is typical LSWR pattern diamond fencing complete with contemporary advertising signs.

The last day's service, 5 February 1955.

**Above -** Prior to departure from Petersfield, Foreman Tupper and Guard L Horwood. The coach used was part of push-pull set No 653.

**Left** - Foreman Tupper again, this time with Driver F M Goldsmith.

Of the two services that operated on the line that day, the crews were:

Train 1 -
Driver   F Goldsmith
Fireman G Howse
Guard   J Hutchinson

Train 2 -
Driver   (Bill) Fears
Fireman J Myers
Guard   L Horwood

*A lowering sky witnesses what would be final train movement through Rogate on the Midhurst to Petersfield railway. The previous day the line had been officially closed but on Sunday 6 February there was an enthusiasts' special working ('The Hampshireman') over the route. A pair of 'E5X' 0-6-2Ts, Nos 32570 and 32576, had been in charge from Horsham to Petersfield, with the pair now seen returning light engine back from Petersfield towards their home shed at Horsham. The combination is seen heading east at Rogate. The station here, 'Rogate for Harting' was well over a mile from either village, the station house built at right angles to the running line. Most of the railway buildings had also been rendered in plaster by this time. By 1955 the former loop platform was long disused, the former signal box having also been downgraded to ground frame status and was now used solely for access to the goods yard. The line here is still in the heart of the Rother Valley much of the route traversed flat with no major engineering problems experienced during construction. The station buildings here remain extant in 2014. Apart from the photographer who recorded the scene, there appears to no one else present.*

**Left -** *Demolition at Elsted c1957. The route remained moribund for some time after February 1955, although it must have come as some surprise when a Matissa Tamping Machine carrying the district engineer made a trip over the line on 4 October 1956. Possibly this was to assess if there was anything worthy of salvage. At Elsted the contractor's crane is in the process of removing the wind pump formerly used to supply water for the station.*

**Bottom -** *Between Petersfield and Rogate. Track lifting near West Heath Common.*

### TO BE CONTINUED...

# THE ILFRACOMBE BRANCH
## Peter Tatlow

Following a visit to the Somerset & Dorset line and walking the line from Radstock to Shepton Mallet to photograph the holiday specials on an August bank holiday, my colleague and I took the local train to Evercreech Junction, where we boarded the train for Highbridge and continued on to Taunton. Rising early on Sunday 3 August 1958, we caught the 8.40am for Exeter St David's, where we changed for a run out to Barnstaple and Ilfracombe, there being no Sunday services on the GW direct line from Taunton to Barnstaple Junction. We returned to the Home Counties that evening.

Barnstaple first achieved a connection with the national rail network in August 1854 by means of the North Devon Railway from Exeter, later to be absorbed into the LSWR. In November 1873 the Devon and Somerset line from Taunton also reached the town. This was initially broad gauge and the two lines remained unconnected until, following gauge conversion in May 1881, the construction of a connecting loop in June 1887 finally allowed through working. The D&S fell into the hands of the GW in 1901, which thereby gave the GWR access to Ilfracombe. The branch to Ilfracombe had been opened on 29 July 1874 and thereafter was taken over by the LSWR. Traffic ceased with the last train on 3 October 1970.

Leaving Barnstaple, the line, just above sea level, parallels the River Taw and is nearly flat as far as Braunton, after which it climbs steeply for six miles, soon rising at the rate of 1 in 40/41, to the summit at Mortehoe at about 600 feet above sea level. After this it drops precipitously for three miles, mainly at 1 in 36 to the station situated high above the town of Ilfracombe. The incline was so steep that, in anticipation, it had led the previous year to the introduction of a class of 0-6-0s known as the 'Ilfracombe Goods'. Controlling ones' descent into Ilfracombe by judicious braking must have been as big a challenge as keeping a grip and not stalling while climbing out.

References
Dendy Marshall CF, *A history of the Southern Railway*, The Southern Railway, 1936, pp 161, 226, 228.
MacDermot, E T, rev'd Clinker C R, *History of Great Western Railway, Vol 2, 1863-1921*, Ian Allan, 1989, pp 91-92.
Parkhouse, N, *The Barnstaple to Ilfracombe line in 1931 - The Brian Perkes Archive*, Railway Archive, No. 41, (Dec 2013), pp 3-28.

*Opposite top and page 43 -* Original 'West Country' class No. 34015 Exmouth *bravely takes six coaches of the 2.20pm Sundays only to Waterloo unassisted out of Ilfracombe and up the 1 in 36 gradient on the way to the summit at Mortehoe on 3 August 1958. The leading two coaches are SR Bulleids in green, while the rest is a four-car set of BR Mark 1s still in carmine and cream.*

*Opposite bottom -* The driver and fireman of No. 34015 give the thumbs up to the line-side photographers, as a keen young spotter looks out of the leading door drop-light. Note the sanders in use.*

*Above -* The last train to Waterloo on a Sunday was the 2.55pm, which needed to convey the photographers to their homes. So having photographed the 2.20pm some way up the line, a quick return to Ilfracombe station was necessary in order to be sure to be aboard. Here No. 34074 46 Squadron *waits at the station with the 2.55pm shortly before departure.*

*Right -* No. 34074 46 Squadron *approaching the summit at Mortehoe with the 2.55pm to Waterloo.*

*This page, above* - *Photographed from the rear of the eight-coach train as No. 34074 gets to grips with the severe pull out of Ilfracombe.*

*This page, left* - *Eight coaches were clearly too much for even a 'West Country', so a Maunsell 2-6-0 N Class assists at the rear to ensure uninterrupted arrival at the summit.*

*Opposite* - *On 2 February 1925, the 10.50 am Horsham to Guildford goods service 'became disabled' at Rudgwick. We are not told what the 'disablement' involved. Assistance was secured using the engine from the 11.35 ex-Guildford 'motor' working, which is seen (above) running back towards the disabled service, and (below) drawing the first part of the disabled train forward before disposing of same in the yard. The process will then be repeated in order to clear the line. This information comes from the records of Edward Wallis who was fortunately on hand to record these images. The engine numbers were not given.*

# RUDGWICK: 2 February 1925

*Above -* Ferry van No. 3 at Dover in the late 1930s. Visible on the underframe are the vacuum and Westinghouse brake cylinders, the dynamo and the four securing eyes for chaining down when on board the ferry. Also seen running over the birdcage lookout is the communication cord rodding. It is in Wagons-Lits blue livery with, in this instance, a not very clean roof.    *A. B. Macleod*

# VARIATIONS ON UTILITY VANS

## Part 3: Passenger Brake Vans and Others

## Mike King

**(Parts 1 and 2 in this series appeared in 'SW' issues 23 and 24 respectively.)**

In part two we looked at the later luggage vans and Covcars plus the bogie vans that did not include accommodation for the guard. Here we will consider those vans specifically designed with a guard's compartment – essential vehicles to allow a van train to run on the system and then move on to a few other non-passenger stock vehicles.

The Southern Railway inherited quite a large stock of passenger brake vans – of four-wheel, six-wheel and bogie types and it was not until 1934 that there was a need to build more. The first requirement came about when the "Night Ferry" was being planned – expected to commence in 1935 but, owing to technical difficulties with the construction of the train ferry dock at Dover, it did not actually start public services until 14 October 1936.

### The Ferry Vans

These were very much "specials" and were unique in a number of very visible respects. Numbered 1-3 in the van list (these numbers now vacated by former LSWR vehicles), they were to Diagram 3091, which describes them as "17-Ton Guard's Vans for Dover Ferry Service". Originally two vans were ordered in March 1934, amended to three in the following August. The design was a stretched version of the luggage van, now 36ft long with a wheelbase of 23ft. Considering that some ex-SECR bogie coaches were only 2 feet longer, this was then a remarkable length for a four-wheeled vehicle. They were dual-braked, steam-heated and were equipped with electric lighting and were ready for service in June 1936.

The most obvious feature was the central raised observatory – not quite a birdcage lookout in the manner of most ex-SECR coaches as this "grew" out of the roof rather than sitting on top and to accommodate this the main roof profile was somewhat flatter than standard – 11ft 7in to crown instead of the usual 12ft. The lookout was necessary to accord with French requirements and the vans were finished in Wagons-Lits blue with a silver-grey roof – to

match the sleeping cars that formed the rest of the through London-Paris portion of the train. They were also labelled "Baggage" – not quite the French spelling – rather than luggage to reinforce their restricted use. Other lettering was in a mix of English and French. Internally the van was divided into a centrally-positioned guard's compartment, with luggage compartments on either side. Because of the dual-braking equipment, there was insufficient room on the underframe for the battery boxes, so these were carried inside one of the luggage compartments.

The Night Ferry service ceased from September 1939 and during World War 2 the vans were released to ordinary traffic, so may have been repainted green with a more simplified lettering layout at some stage; however No. 2 was noted in grey livery in September 1945. The ferry service was not immediately reinstated after the war as the three train ferry ships took some time to be demobilised and it was not until December 1947 that they returned to the duty. British Railways lettering was later applied and the vans continued in use until September 1960, when they no longer conformed to Continental regulations. In October 1960 they all had their Westinghouse brakes and several other ferry fittings removed and were repainted green, now simply considered as standard 4-wheeled passenger brakes and given the British Railways code BY – just like the other 255 more ordinary brakes yet to be described. The author recalls being surprised to see No. 2 pass through Surbiton in a Waterloo-Basingstoke train in 1961, freshly repainted green. They might now turn up anywhere on any service and were no longer granted any special treatment. Nos. 1 & 2 were withdrawn in 1969 but van 3 lasted until July 1974 – by then stripped of lighting and in use just as an ordinary luggage van with the guard's compartment out of use. None ever regained blue livery under British Rail.

### Four-wheeled Passenger Brakes

Following on from the Ferry vans, it was not a difficult task to turn the design into something more suitable for ordinary

---

*Opposite bottom - Van S3S again, at London Bridge in 1967, now in green livery and long past its ferry days. The Westinghouse gear has gone, as has the communication cord rodding. This shows the other side of the van, without the small guard's window. The guard's door is inset 4½ inches from the side planking. These were the only SR passenger brake vans to be evenly planked.*

*H. V. Tumilty*

| Running Nos | Date Built | Remarks |
|---|---|---|
| 400-449 | Ashford 6-7/37 | Some were stove fitted |
| 651-750 | Ashford/Eastleigh 3-9/38 | |
| 751-800 | Eastleigh 3-10/39 | |
| 931-980 | Eastleigh 10/40-1/41 | Some later news vans |
| 10-14 | Eastleigh 4/41 | Safe fitted. Diagram 3094 |

van trains. Known to the Southern Railway as "Van C"; 255 of these were completed between June 1937 and April 1941 in five batches. Diagrams 3092 and 3094 were allocated and they were rated at 16-tons. Details are as shown in the table above.

The different batches gave rise to some minor livery variations but it is not known how many (or if any) were actually painted in either Dover or malachite green. Underframes were often completed at Ashford or Lancing and run to Eastleigh for bodywork finishing. The British

Railways code was BY (B for brake, Y to signify four-wheeled).

Just which ones were stove-fitted (and when) is confusing. Nos. 400-442 were equipped with stoves at dates between March 1938 and February 1939 and could be distinguished by an orange (sometimes later yellow) eaves panel at each end of the side, while later an orange (or yellow) door panel was added. Nos. 420-434 had their stoves removed in 1946 but they were refitted again to vans 420-430 in 1966-68, only for them to be removed from all vans yet again soon after as the guards were then refusing to

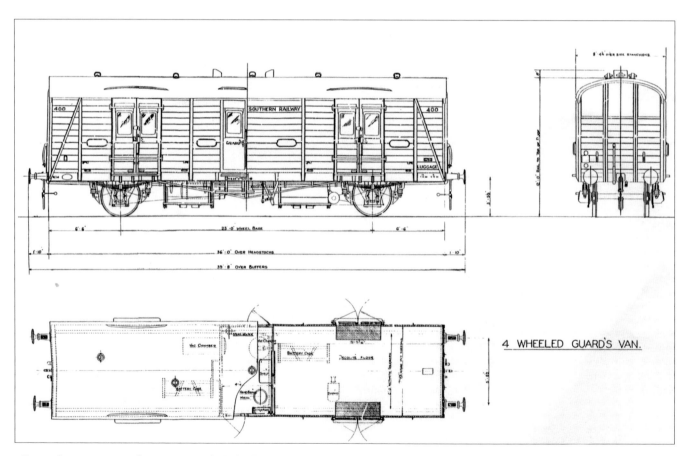

*General arrangement drawing No. E27548, showing the standard Van C and dated December 1936. Roof periscopes have replaced the birdcage lookout and a normal roof profile has been used. On that score the drawing is perhaps a little inaccurate in its portrayal of the roof shape but it shows short steps below the guard's door and also even planking. None of the vans was so constructed! The lettering layout is shown, but does not yet include the letters XP and WB 23ft 0in, added in white over the word 'Luggage'.*

*A view at Guildford, taken from near the tunnel mouth, about mid-1939. Q class 0-6-0 No. 543 shunts past the signal cabin but two Van Cs may be seen in the sidings, showing slightly different liveries. At right is van 743, new in June 1938 as part of order A974 and lettered "Southern Railway", while on the left van 797 dates from May 1939 as part of order A1030 and is just lettered "Southern". The base colours look quite different – so what shades of green were they? Note also the slightly different position of the numbers and the grey chalking slates.*
*F. E. Box*

travel in what they now considered sub-standard accommodation! Removal dates for Nos. 435-442 do not seem to be recorded but according to carriage working notices none of these had them by 1945. The stove-fitted vans had their workings closely controlled and most were used in van trains, where steam heating would otherwise not be available. If the van were attached to a passenger train, this would not be a problem. These vans were not supposed to work off the Southern but this restriction was somewhat relaxed after nationalisation. Vans 400/1 were provided with side lamp irons for working in West of England goods trains – taking in regular Exeter-Plymouth workings and some trips as far east as Axminster. The two vans stayed on these duties until September 1964 but the lamp irons remained on them until scrapping. Non-stove-fitted vans 660/61 were roof-boarded for Messrs Aplin & Barrett's dairy traffic "To work between Yeovil & Derby", running via Templecombe and the S&DJR until August 1939 – it is not clear if this traffic resumed after the war but some carriage working notices of the late 1940s continue to show the allocation.

When new, some vans were lettered "Southern Railway" in full, while later ones omitted the word "Railway". The 2+2 planking appeared first on these vans – some time before its usage began on covered goods and brake vans. Frank Foote recorded No. 437 in malachite in

July 1942 – the only one specifically noted – but Nos. 400/4/8/11/21 were all seen in grey with orange eaves and door panels at dates between November 1942 and May 1946, while non-stove-fitted vans 659, 709 and 958 were also noted grey in 1943. Van 681 was badly damaged by enemy action on 28th May 1941 but was repaired and returned to traffic in January 1942 – at least three others suffered similar but less extensive damage and were repaired rather more quickly.

The five safe-fitted vans to Diagram 3094 were the last to be constructed and were ordered as replacements for six ex-SECR safe-fitted birdcage passenger brake vans but by the time they entered traffic, the duties on which they were to be used had ceased under wartime conditions so all five were placed at the ends of LSWR "long" sets of bogie coaches used for troop train work, to cover a shortage of suitable brake third vehicles. Set numbers were 303/4 (two vans in each) and 305 (one end only). This was a rare occurrence where a utility van was allocated a set number, but van 974 was later seen at the end of SECR "long" set 334, deputising for a birdcage corridor brake composite. After 1945 the intended duties for the safe-fitted vans failed to reappear and they were not allocated any specific workings. However, to draw attention to their status, the van number was written in large white numerals on a red panel – similar to how the SECR safe vans had been

*Stove-equipped van S402 at Clapham Yard on 17 August 1952. This has orange (or yellow?) eaves panels with the number superimposed directly onto them, complete with freshly added "S" prefix. Assuming these to be yellow, it is reasonable to assume the panels are orange. In SR days the plank carrying the number would often have been green, breaking up the panel somewhat. On the door, the word "Guard" and 402 are in black. The livery is either Maunsell or malachite green.*

*J. H. Aston*

*Newspaper van BY S961S roof-boarded "Newspapers London Ashford Margate", probably at Rotherhithe Road carriage sidings (the R. RD chalk marking is the giveaway) about 1957/8 – probably in crimson lake livery. Typically it is in a train of other utility vans.*

*The Lens of Sutton Association*

*N class Mogul No. 31847 heads the 10.46am Tavistock-Plymouth Friary goods at Mutley in June 1955, with stove van S400S as the leading vehicle – part of the circuit working for the van which had left Exeter Central at 2.20am. One of the side lamp irons may just be seen low down on the leading corner post. The loco will have left Exmouth Junction around 6am and spent some time shunting at Yeoford before continuing westwards at 9.30am.* R. E. Vincent, cty The Transport Treasury

*Safe-fitted BY No. S12 at Clapham Junction on 26ᵗ July 1950. The large white numerals and red panel may be seen, as is the safe compartment just to the right of the guard's door. Also note plywood PMV No. S1617 with left-hand numbering and code on a crimson finish – how the vans were first painted in BR livery.* D. Cullum/The Lens of Sutton Association

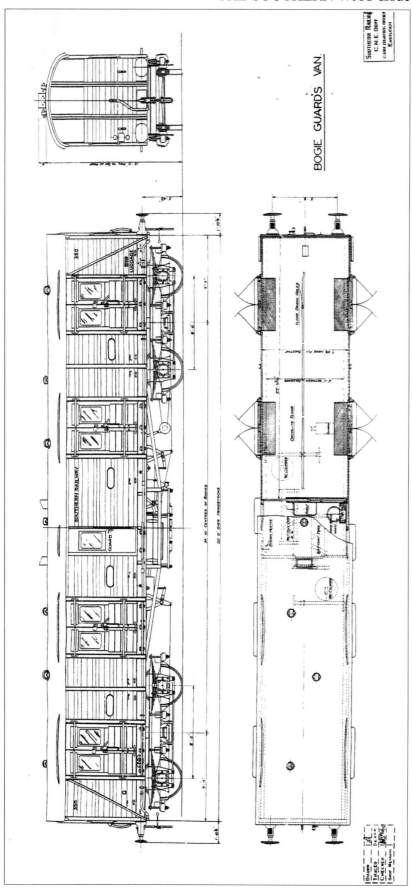

BOGIE GUARD'S VAN.

annotated before 1940. Once BR crimson lake livery was applied this became a blue panel. The safe itself was simply a box-like enclosure that stretched right across the van, with no internal access. Externally, all that could be seen was a square steel door, accessible using nothing more sophisticated than a standard carriage door key. The guard's compartment was larger on these vans than on the standard vans, with a corresponding reduction in luggage space.

Once in British Railways ownership, crimson livery began to be applied from 1949, while vans 937/43/52/56/61/65/72/79 were roof-boarded for newspaper traffic in 1955/6 – being used on Waterloo-West of England services and some South Eastern section duties until 1964. BR green livery gradually replaced crimson lake from 1956, while a few may have carried rail blue after 1966 – although these seem to have been very much in the minority. Apart from van 777, totally destroyed in an accident at Witham on 7th March 1950, general withdrawal began in 1966 and was completed with van 713 in August 1978. Safe van 14 was withdrawn in 1969 and transferred to Swindon Works as an "Enparts" van, but the other four lasted to the mid-1970s. Van 938 was modified in June 1965 as a "high security van for GPO use". Externally both guard's doors and the left-hand pair of double doors on each side were removed and planked over, flush with the rest of the side sheeting, while steel sheets replaced the remaining pairs of droplight windows. All this work was done meticulously and exactly matched the rest of the 2+2 planking. Internally a lavatory was provided in the former guard's compartment. Diagram 3095 was allocated. This van was then used on the overnight Waterloo-Portsmouth mail train until 1971. After withdrawal the van was stored at Micheldever until 1976, pending possible departmental conversion, but this never took place. The rest ceased to be guard's vans around 1969 – then being used purely as luggage, parcels or newspaper vans.

*General arrangement drawing E27749, dated April 1937 showing the Van B. This does correctly show the 2+2 planking and the original lettering layout.*

*The official portrait of Van B No. 359 when new in September 1938 and likely to be finished in Maunsell green livery.*
*This van ran until September 1978 but the record is held by No. 399 – from September 1938 until August 1986.*

SR Official

Eight vans were modified after withdrawal as Civil Engineer's departmental staff and tool brake vans, being renumbered into the BR DB975XXX series and repainted ED olive green, while a few others entered departmental or internal use at various locations, not necessarily all being on the Southern Region. Safe-fitted van 13 was purchased by the Swanage Railway, while many of the ordinary vans are also now in preservation. Indeed, one sold to the Bluebell Railway in 1972 had been withdrawn due to "serious electrical defects". This turned out to be a broken dynamo drive belt, so someone wangled a bargain!!

**Bogie Brake Vans**

At the same time as the first Van Cs were ordered (May 1936) authorisation was also given for 50 bogie luggage vans to be constructed. This was amended 12 months later to include guard's accommodation but it was some time before construction commenced. A total of 130

were built in three batches. Allocated Diagram 3093, they were officially described as 28-ton bogie passenger brake vans but were known universally by their code as "Van B", both in Southern and BR days. For anyone wondering, "Van A" was a standard 10 or 12-ton covered goods wagon with vacuum brakes. Numbering details are as the table below.

Apart from some very minor planking details (all had 2+2 planks) and a change of position of the brake gear on the underframes of the final batch, all were practically identical and were a stretched version of the four-wheelers. Again, original liveries are a moot point – the first batch was lettered in Maunsell style with the words "Southern Railway" in full, probably on Maunsell green. The second batch is likely to just have the word "Southern" but on what colour green is uncertain. The BR batch appeared in crimson livery with pale yellow lettering – and all liveries had black ends. Frank Foote noted No. 212 in grey in June 1943 but a month later it had been outshopped in malachite.

| Running Nos | Date Built | Remarks |
|---|---|---|
| 350-399 | Eastleigh 8-10/38 | Some later stove-fitted |
| 201-250 | Eastleigh 11-12/39 | Some later stove-fitted |
| 251-280 | Lancing 11/52-2/53 | Some later news vans |

*Stove-fitted Van B S390 in green with orange panels on 9ʳ July 1950 – in a line of similar vehicles – no. 375 to the left, 387 to the right. Livery exactly as Van C 402 seen in earlier picture.* Author's Collection

No. 372 was seen in grey in July 1946 while No. 217 was noted freshly painted malachite in April 1946, yet 394 was specifically recorded as freshly repainted dark green in November 1944.

Stove fitting is almost as complicated as on the Van Cs. Vans 395-99 were stove-equipped by 1944, while Nos. 380-94 were equipped during 1946/7 – quite possibly using the stoves taken from Van Cs 420-434 so maybe the guards had complained that the four-wheelers were rough riders. Nos. 370-79 were fitted in December 1948-February 1949, while vans 368/69 were done as recently as 1962. Of the later vans, Nos. 201-3/5-31 were stove-equipped in 1966 -68, mostly for Central and South Eastern section workings, but van 204 was excluded because by then it was permanently allocated to the Scottish Region for the Kyle of Lochalsh line. Like the Van Cs, these also received orange or yellow eaves/door panels and had their duties listed in carriage working notices.

Nos. 265-280 were roof-boarded as newspaper vans in 1953/4 for the South Western section and 14 had two-day diagrams allocated – most involving the 1.15am Waterloo-West of England newspaper train (seven in use each night with return to London at various times over the following 24 hours) with two vans spare to cover routine maintenance. At first each was roof-boarded for its allotted destination but by about 1960 these boards were removed

and the vans were more simply stencilled "Newspapers-Waterloo-West of England", allowing them to be switched about more readily. As the traffic declined only vans 272-80 remained so allocated until around 1975, after which just two South Eastern section duties remained until 1977. Two vans were allocated to a permanent set formation around 1955 – at each end of SECR birdcage stock set 696 – but their identities are not known.

Like the BYs, the Van Bs began to lose their brake van status from 1969 – again because the guards were refusing to ride in them, so those with stoves gradually had these removed. Van 204 was still exiled in Scotland and remained a passenger brake but only nos. 225-30 retained guard's van status until 1974 on the Southern Region; taking in duties that embraced the South Eastern section – in particular those traversing the Hastings direct line. The others also had their lighting stripped out and were then classed simply as luggage or parcels vans. The first to receive rail blue was van 220 in December 1966. The first withdrawals also took place in that year but by far the majority survived until BR ceased its parcels collection and delivery service in June 1981, after which withdrawals gathered pace. By then quite a number were painted rail blue. However, until the Hastings line was electrified and the restriction on using 9ft wide stock was lifted, these vans were still needed for SE division services and so 30 were

*Van B No. S234S in Southern Region green livery at Axminster on 19ᵗʰ April 1963, showing the standard post-1955 lettering layout and the "B" coding above the number. This was one from the second batch, running from November 1939 until July 1981.*                    *A. E.West*

kept in stock from 1982 onwards. Electrification of the route was completed in May 1986 when certain sections of line through the various tunnels were re-laid as single track, allowing BR Mk1 stock to be used and the final six Van Bs (Nos. 236/52/54/65/76 and 399) were withdrawn in August and September 1986. These were the very last SR utility vans to remain in ordinary traffic, bringing to an end a chapter that began almost 70 years previously. Some vans entered departmental or internal use, while odd ones have been grounded and a number are now in the hands of the preservation movement – again a few are expected to be used purely for their underframes which, at 50ft over headstocks are eminently suitable for mounting pre-Grouping coach bodies upon.

**Special Cattle Vans**

Strictly speaking, these do not fit the utility van mould but were contemporary with them; hence they will also be described. The Southern inherited 96 special or prize cattle vans from the pre-Grouping companies, used not for ordinary animals but for prize breeds etc, when attending agricultural shows and the like. Pre-Grouping opinion differed regarding whether to classify them as passenger or goods stock, but the Southern decided on the former and

they received green livery after 1923. Several, particularly those of LBSCR and SER origin, were already elderly and had no accommodation for a groom to accompany the animals. It was therefore decided to replace these with some more up-to-date vehicles. Accordingly, 20 vans were authorised in April 1929 but this was soon increased to 50 – all being built by Birmingham Railway Carriage & Wagon Company in 1930, allowing 50 of the older pre-Grouping examples to be rapidly withdrawn – including one of Somerset & Dorset Joint line origin and about 18 ex-LSWR ones in addition to the aforementioned Brighton and South Eastern vans.

They were 26ft long with a wheelbase of 17ft 6in – but had a plain arc-roof profile instead of the semi-elliptical roof of other utility vans. They were dual-braked but the Westinghouse gear was removed during 1933. There was a central compartment for the groom with cattle compartments at each end. Running numbers were 3679-3728 while Diagram 3141 was allocated and their telegraphic code was "Catox". This code did not appear on the vans themselves. In appearance they could be mistaken for a horsebox – not that the Southern built any – and sometimes their occupants were racehorses. When travelling circuses presented themselves, the occupants

*Special cattle van 3683, officially photographed by Birmingham Railway Carriage & Wagon Company in June 1930. Maunsell green with black ends and yellow lettering (including the 12"high company letters). The door droplight is grained teak but this would have probably been repainted green at first overhaul. The vertical sliding shutters are in the raised (closed) position at this end, lowered (open) position at the far end. It had oil lighting with end steps and handrail for access.*
*BRCW/SR Official.*

could be a little more exotic – kangaroos being pictured in one Southern Railway Magazine article!

The vehicles would be stabled at certain locations – especially those such as Salisbury, Chichester, Guildford or Ashford, where regular markets were situated and they might be seen singly on the front or rear of a passenger train or in a trainload if a complete farm needed to be removed from one part of the country to another. During World War 2 and after, some were noted in pale grey livery (including Nos. 3687, 3700/4), while after 1949 British Railways crimson lake was applied, replaced by green after 1956, although quite a number were scrapped still in red livery in the early 1960s. Only van 3697 has been recorded in malachite – in July 1941 and again in November 1944.

After Nationalisation the Southern Region found itself with ten of the pre-Grouping special cattle vans still on the books and it was decided to replace these with ten more of Southern design. They were authorised on 12th September 1950 but construction did not take place until September/October 1952. Apart from the provision of electric lighting instead of oil lamps, they were identical to

the 1930 vans and were allocated numbers 3729-38 and coded SCV. These appeared in crimson lake with red ends from new. Just how much they were needed is debateable and they might just have been ordered to give Lancing some extra work (such things did occur in the early days of BR ownership) – the fact that it took two years to get around to building them tends to reinforce this view. Indeed, not so many years later the traffic in livestock declined rapidly, such that all the original vans were withdrawn from traffic in 1961-63 – largely en bloc – so probably at the accountant's bidding but one suspects that many had performed few duties in their final years. Quite a few were sold for their bodies to be used as farm stables – this was most common in Scotland and six are recorded as being sold from Inverurie Works during 1963; perhaps giving an indication of where they saw most use in their final years. The author does not recall ever seeing one on the move – only stored in sidings. The BR-built vans were retained for a little longer but even these succumbed between 1966 and 1972. During their last years most were stored at

*SCV No. S3729S – the first of the BR-built batch when new at Lancing Works in September 1952, in crimson lake with black ends. They had electric lighting with dynamo and battery box on the underframe and no end steps or handrails provided – otherwise they were identical to the 1930 vans. This shows the opposite side to No. 3683. The vehicle was officially withdrawn in December 1970 but was not actually deleted from stock lists until August 1971 – almost certainly stored at Micheldever during this time.* BR Official

Sturminster Newton, Blandford Forum, Salisbury and finally Micheldever.

Two were much rebuilt as train heating boiler vans Nos. DS70190/91, having largely new bodywork provided. In this form both lasted to the 1980s, firstly at Bournemouth West and Weymouth, latterly at Oxford. One of the 1952 vans, No. 3733 has been taken into the National Collection at York Museum and after many years of storage was restored in 2004 and may now be seen at Shildon.

**Some "might-have-beens"**

Inevitably, a few designs were proposed – in some instances actually ordered – but changed circumstances required a rethink. There is an intriguing pencil entry in the Lancing register against van numbers 1041/42, for two hearse vans to replace the pair of LSWR vehicles on the Brookwood Necropolis service. Order No. 1032 was placed on 14th June 1938 for these, but before construction took place the war intervened and the Necropolis station outside Waterloo was badly damaged by bombing. The service was suspended for the rest of the war but never resumed. The order was finally cancelled in May 1945. Just whether a design was prepared is not known but it would be interesting to ponder on what form of utility van variation might have been produced. This was not the only design where vehicle numbers were actually reserved.

As noted earlier, the Southern did not build any true horseboxes – instead continuing to rely on the considerable stock of pre-Grouping vehicles right through until the last was withdrawn in 1959. However, perhaps as many as four batches of horseboxes – each of 25 vehicles – were ordered in May 1939, April 1940, April 1941 and April 1942, although it is possible that the last two were carryovers of the first two orders. Numbers 2861-85 were allocated to the first batch but again no construction took place and the orders were finally cancelled in 1945. No drawings are known but the existing special cattle van design would have sufficed – but whether this would have been to Bulleid's liking is anybody's guess.

One final design exists just as a drawing – with no order to substantiate it. This was for a pure Bulleid vehicle and is described as a baggage car for special trains – drawing No. L8838. This shows a 64ft 6in long Bulleid corridor coach with four pairs of double doors on each side, without guard's accommodation but having a row of toplight windows along each side. It might have been traditionally constructed or might even have had plywood bodywork like Bulleid's rather remarkable sleeping saloon No. 100s. The drawing is not dated, nor is there any indication of how many were proposed. However, it illustrates that Bulleid's ideas, had they been enacted, would have been very different to that of the Maunsell/Lynes utility van designs.

# SOUTHERN RAILWAY TRAFFIC OFFICERS CONFERENCE:

## Minutes of a meeting held at Waterloo Station on Monday 28 March 1938 chaired by Gilbert Szlumper CBE General Manager

## (Notes compiled by David Monk-Steel)

### 10333 Fatal Accidents to Railway Servants

Stewarts Lane 22 December 1937 a Sandman who was engaged in turning sand at the furnace suffered burns to his left foot which necessitated his absence from work and was removed to hospital some time later where his left leg was amputated because of dry gangrene, and on the 16 January 1938 he passed away.

### 10334 Fatal Accidents to Members of the Public

Between 22 January and 22 of February 1938 19 fatal accidents to members of the public occurred on the Southern Railway. Nine were attributed to suicide by stepping in front of a moving train, two more were unexplained but may have been suicide, three were pedestrians struck by trains on foot crossings, one was a trespasser struck by a train, one was an off-duty porter who, after leaving work suffered a brain haemorrhage on his way home, one passenger fell down footbridge stairs, one was a contractor's foreman walking along a steel joist when he was struck on the head by a plank and fell to his death, and one passenger who attempted to board a moving train who fell between the train and the platform.

### 10335 Accidents to Trains

a) Between Erith and Slade Green, 28 January 1938. A wagon which was being shunted out of the 12:45 am freight train from Lower Sydenham was derailed at North End sidings blocking the down line. When detaching the guards van a breakaway occurred between the 23rd and 24th wagon and the 23rd wagon was derailed and the 24th wagon sustained a broken drawbar.

b) New Cross 2 February 1938. The 4:35 pm Hammersmith to New Cross electric train came into slight contact with the buffers in the East London line platform.

c) Parks Bridge Junction and Hither Green 2 February 1938. At 10:15 pm when the 8:10 pm LNER freight train from Hornsey East Yard to Hither Green Sidings consisting of 24 wagons and a 20-ton brake van, was passing Parks Bridge Junction two pairs of wheels of an LNER bogie wagon conveying portions of a gantry from Carlisle to Woolwich Arsenal became derailed to the off side at the trailing end of No. 24 points and re-railed themselves 100 yards later. 998 yards further the leading bogie again became derailed. The driver brought the train to a stand opposite Hither Green 'B' signal box. An impedance bond and two axle boxes of the wagon sustained damage. On examination it appeared that the load had shifted and unbalanced the wagon, probably because the chains securing it were slack and no scotches had been in place to prevent it moving sideways. The LNER accepted that the load had not been secured properly.

d) Bournemouth Central 7 February 1938. At 5:28am M7 class No 57 en-route light between Bournemouth Central to Bournemouth West, collided with a push-pull set standing opposite the signal box. The fireman sustained minor injuries. An empty train composed of three carriages plus a two coach push-pull set had arrived on the down local line at 5:6 am and shunted to the down through line via the scissor crossing. The front set to form the 7:0 am to Brockenhurst was detached and was taken to the western end of the station, and back over 47 crossover to the up local, the rear set to form the 5:47 am to Swanage with tail lamp attached was left on the down through line. The booked locomotive for the Swanage train had encountered difficulty in attaching so the light engine to Bournemouth West was given priority. However the signalman had forgotten the push-pull set, failed to apply lever collar reminder appliances and cleared 27 shunt signal and the down through starting signal No 4. The driver and fireman of the light engine failed to locate the tail light of the push-pull set in the dark and were unable to stop before a collision occurred. The push-pull set was driven forward by the collision 20 yards and sustained considerable damage.

e) Clapham Junction 10 February 1938. At 11:40 am 'H' class No. 1329 hauling a 6-wheeled van passed the middle siding (between the up Windsor local and from Kensington arrival) 91 shunt signal at danger and became derailed all wheels on the catch points. The van was also derailed one pair of wheels. The fireman apparently misread the Up

## BOURNEMOUTH CENTRAL.

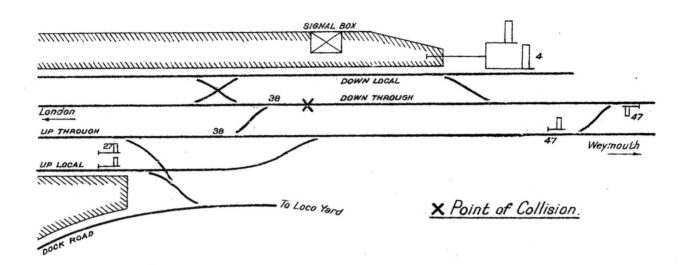

**X** *Point of Collision.*

## CLAPHAM JUNCTION.

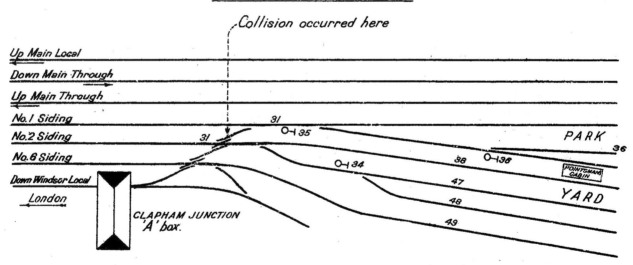

Windsor local line signal as applying to the move and misinformed his driver that it was all right to proceed.

f) Clapham Junction 15 February 1938. At 11:3 pm M7 class No. 667 collided with O2 class No. 179 at No. 31 crossover between No 1 and No 2 sidings. It was discovered on enquiry that the pointsman had failed to check that there was no conflicting movement before authorising the shunter to make a move from No. 36 siding to the Windsor line.

g) Calstock 16 February 1938. At 12:40 pm, during shunting, locomotive No. 758 became derailed on points at the Gunnislake end of the station obstructing the single line. On arrival of the early running 12:40 pm freight from Bere Alston to Hingston down siding the vehicles were left on the single line alongside the platform whilst the engine proceeded into the yard for shunting. On completion the locomotive was returning to the train with one wagon via No.4 points but the wagon was still foul of No. 4 points when the signalman required to normalise them, and despite trying to move them they did not complete their travel, and

*On Friday 28 June 1957 an accident occurred during what is believed to have been a shunting move at Clapham Junction. As is well known in history, the ability of wooden-bodied stock allied to conventional screw couplings was not good at withstanding impact and telescoping was the inevitable result. Here former LSW non-corridor vehicles S164S and S166S have come to grief. No formal accident report appears to exist for the incident and so we may hopefully assume the vehicles were indeed empty at the time.*

*R F Roberts*

they were standing half open at the moment when the driver decided to proceed back on to his train without proper authority.

h) Charing Cross 17 February 1938. At 12:59 pm the locomotive of the 11:15 am from Hasting came into contact with the buffers in platform 5. The driver was held responsible for an error of judgement.

i) Salisbury 3 March 1938. At 7:58 am GWR Bogie 'Macaw' wagon loaded with 5 tons of reinforcing bar from Newport (Mon) to Bournemouth was derailed at No 32 West box points at the connection from the GWR to the up local. The train had been standing astride No.32 points awaiting the passage of 7:52 am from Salisbury to Portsmouth, and in anticipation of making a further empty coaching stock movement the signalman erroneously operated the points under the wagon, and when subsequently the freight train was to be moved, the rear bogie was directed to the wrong line and became derailed. After extensive tests the GWR wagon was found to fail to have operated the protecting track circuit and further tests have been initiated with the GWR.

j) Strawberry Hill 5 March 1938. At 2:6 pm the 1:42 pm 8-car empty electric train from Shepperton to Strawberry Hill collided with the engine of the 11:36am freight from Strawberry Hill to Feltham in No 2 siding. The electric train was due to go into No 4 siding, but the porter had omitted to operate the points for the arrival.

*Early 1930s main line service. A Victoria to Bognor express working at Dorking North c1932.*

*Dr Ian C Allen*

k) Orpington 16 March 1938. At 6:49 am the 6:9 am 8-coach electric train from Holborn to Orpington came into contact with the up bay platform. Only slight damage was caused.

## 10336 Irregularities in Working

The following signals were passed at danger without authority:

10 February 1938. Penge West down local home locomotive 1820 (light) by 1858 yards.

10 February 1938. Queens Road (Battersea) down Windsor outer WD46 8:30m (elec) Waterloo to Teddington by 90 yards.

21 February 1938. Loco. Junction Down main through to sidings auxiliary WC16 Light engine 751 by 100 yards.

21 February 1938. Three Bridges Horsham branch home 7:45 am. Bognor to Victoria by 20 yards.

25 February 1938. Walton up through home 4.52 pm, Torrington to Nine Elms by 200 yards.

26 February 1938. Portslade down home 12:34 pm (elec) Brighton to West Worthing by 30 yards.

28 February 1938. Brighton up east branch home 11:44 am (elec) Seaford to Brighton by 20 yards.

1 March 1938. Norwood Junction north down local home 7:31 am (elec) London Bridge to London Bridge via Norwood Junction and Tulse Hill by 33 yards.

5 March 1938. Keymer Crossing (Wivelsfield) down outer home CG2 8:30 am (elec) Horsted Keynes to Seaford by 40 yards.

5 March 1938. Woking up local outer home WV45 8:10am am (elec) Alton to Waterloo by 20 yards.

*Norwood Junction with examples of contemporary motive power from the 1930s.*

8 March 1938. Gatwick Racecourse down local home CM4511:45 am (empty elec) Selhurst to Gatwick Racecourse by 170 yards.

8 March 1938. Purley North down main inner home 6:16 am (elec) London Bridge to Brighton by 30 yards.

8 March 1938. Walton up through advanced starter 7:35am Bournemouth to Waterloo by 40 yards.

13 March 1938. Balham intermediate down local home 9:48 pm (elec) Victoria to Epsom Downs by 636 yards.

15 March 1938. Haywards Heath up through advance starter 7:28 am. (elec) Brighton to London Bridge.
Other irregularities

23 February 1938 between Waldron and Horam to Heathfield the 4:39pm from Eastbourne to Tunbridge Wells proceeded through the section without the electric train staff.

**10337   Fires on Company Premises**
12 February 1938 between Waterloo and Vauxhall adjacent to the up Windsor line a PW hut was gutted.

16 February 1938 near East Croydon, a fire in the gangway connection of the 9:5 am Victoria to Portsmouth between 3rd class Pullman No 23 and coach 5643. Extinguished by staff

minor damage only.

27 February 1938 between Fleet and Winchfield, a fire in the gangway of the 11:30 am Waterloo to Bournemouth West in Restaurant Car 7952, extinguished by staff.

5 March 1938 between Streatham and Tulse Hill, fire in cable troughing attended to by the fire brigade.

10 March 1938 at 2:56 pm between Swanley and St. Mary Cray, serious fire reported by a passenger in rear two coaches of 11:47am Minster to Victoria. Train stopped by communication cord at Bournewood Crossing, and train crew attempted to extinguish. Passengers in rear two carriages detrained or moved forward to the leading two vehicles which were uncoupled and drawn clear. The local fire brigade was summoned but was unable to prevent destruction of the bodywork of rear two carriages. The 2:35 pm Hither Green to Ashford freight train stopped by hand signal from the passenger train driver but came to a stand alongside the burning carriages, and had to restart quickly to prevent fire from spreading to the trucks. One wagon was scorched. The front two carriages were detached and drawn off and took the passengers to St. Mary Cray where they completed their journey by alternative services

The fire is believed to have started in the gangway of coach 5537 which was the third vehicle. The burning carriages were shunted into Bournewood siding by light engine sent from Swanley. The Ground Frame at Bournewood was also damaged by fire.

## 10338 Gales

A gale occurred on 12 February 1938 and the following incidents were recorded as a consequence:

Strood Tunnel flooded between 11:10 pm and 12:55 am as a result of the River Medway overflowing at Strood Dock. Subsequently a speed restriction was imposed.

Between Stoke Junction and Grain Crossing a portion of the sea wall had collapsed and ballast was being washed away. Repairs took two days while the line had to be blocked.

A tree was blown down on to the railway between West Norwood and Gypsy Hill. The 7 pm freight from Old Oak Common to Norwood was stopped clear of the obstruction.

## 10339 Ice on Conductor Rails

Heavy delays occurred between Three Bridges and Balcombe tunnel on the evening of Tuesday 15 February 1938 due to arcing caused by ice on the conductor rails damaged the current collecting equipment on trains.

## 10340 Obstructions on the line

a) 4 February 1938 between Fort Brockenhurst and Gosport, at 5:36 pm the 4:26 pm pull and push train from Alton to Gosport formed of two coaches with engine propelling ran through and damaged the gates at Cambridge Road level crossing. Leading coach 6496 sustained damage. The crossing keeper was held responsible for failing to attend to his duties by not having his gates open in sufficient time for the train, the driver and guard were also held responsible for failing to keep a good look out.

b) 5 February 1938, at 1:15 pm near Canterbury East the guard of 12:20 pm Snowdown Colliery to Hoo Junction freight train which was standing in Canterbury East down sidings observed that a tree had blown across the up line with the 12:26 pm Dover Marine to Faversham passenger train approaching. He ran 100 yards exhibiting a hand danger signal and was successful in bringing the passenger train to a halt before reaching the obstruction. The tree was on private land and was being felled at the time of the occurrence. GPO telephone cables were damaged by the tree as it fell. The guard has been commended for his prompt action with a reward of £1 for his vigilance.

c) 14 February 1938, at 10:37 pm at Addlestone a motor car struck the gates of the level crossing dislodging and damaging them and in turn being struck by 10:33 pm (elec) Weybridge to Staines. The car driver was found to be under the influence of alcohol and has been arrested by the local police.

d) 22 February 1938, at Tangley level crossing the 3:30 am Redhill to Reading freight train passed the signal protecting Tangley crossing at danger and collided with and damaged both gates. The over-run of the signal which was 50 yards from the crossing was approximately half a mile. The train had previously been stopped between Reigate and Betchworth to extinguish a fire in the third wagon from the engine which was loaded with pipes packed with straw.

e) 26 February 1938 between Waddon and Wallington, at 1:32 pm the Company's telegraph wires were severed by an aircraft which made a forced landing in a field alongside the railway. All communication was lost but trains continued to be run under 'time interval' working. The pilot and two other persons suffered injuries and were removed to hospital. )

f) 28 February 1938 at Small Bridge level crossing (between Horsmonden and Goudhurst), the 7:25 pm train from Paddock Wood to Hawkhurst came into contact and badly damaged the down side gate of the crossing. The crossing keeper's wife was operating the gates whilst he took a break. She closed the gates to road but failed to padlock them. It is assumed that someone passed the gates after they had been shut, and left the gate foul of the line.

## 10341  Burglaries

Between 6 and 28 February 1938 15 burglaries on SR premised occurred. Five were to automatic vending machines, five were to shops or tobacco kiosks, and of the rest a staff lobby, a booking office, a coal order office, a refreshment room and a goods shed were burgled.

## 10342  Mishaps to Road Vehicles

A 'knock for knock' agreement has been signed with the National Farmers Union Mutual insurance in respect of horses and vehicles.

## 10343  Compensation claims (goods and passenger)

£4,529 15s 11d was paid in February 1938, compared to £4,152 9s 10d in the equivalent period in 1937.

## 10344  Demurrage and Siding Rent on Merchandise (other than coal and Coke)  raised against traders on wagons and sheets. - *see summary table below.*

| Outstanding from previous month | Charges Raised during the month | Collected during the month | Amount cleared during the month | Outstanding at end of month |
|---|---|---|---|---|
| £1896 14s 11d | £915 9s 1d | £610 11s 1d | £147 8s 3d | £2054 4s 8d |

**10345 Outstandings (Goods & Parcels) including Continental and Channel Islands traffic**
A summary of outstanding accounts was submitted.

**10346 Surplus Cash and Losses in Booking**
A net loss of £10 9s 9d was recorded.

**10347 Bad Debts**
Two new bad debtors were notified.

**10348 Engine Failures** - *see table opposite.*
Four weeks ended 19 February 1938 compared with corresponding period in 1937.

**10349 Mileage**
Four weeks ended 19 February 1938
**Steam Locomotive Engines (including Sentinel and Petrol Cars)**

| Locomotive Division | Number of Failures | |
|---|---|---|
| | 1938 | 1937 |
| Western | 12 | 14 |
| Eastern | 16 | 18 |
| Total | 26 | 32 |
| Miles run per failure | 125671 | 114553 |

| TRAIN MILES | |
|---|---|
| Coaching | |
| Passenger Loaded | |
| Ordinary | 1778551 |
| Special and Conditional | 31567 |
| Fruit, Milk, Fish etc. loaded | |
| Ordinary | 115052 |
| Special and Conditional | 9542 |
| Empty | 44788 |
| Freight | |
| Ordinary | 529567 |
| Special and Conditional | 27223 |
| | |
| Total Train Miles | 2536190 |
| | |
| OTHER MILES | |
| Shunting | |
| Coaching | 152735 |
| Freight | 526109 |
| | |
| Assisting Required | |
| Coaching | 3549 |
| Freight | 3377 |
| Assisting not required | 8365 |
| Light | 191323 |
| | |
| DEPARTMENTAL MILES | |
| Locomotive Department | 45736 |
| Carriage and Wagon Department | 11608 |
| Stores Department | 245 |
| Ballasting (including Engineers Service Trains) | 74591 |
| Miscellaneous | 2857 |

**Electric Trains**

| TRAIN MILES | |
|---|---|
| Ordinary | |
| Loaded | |
| Western (excluding Waterloo and City Railway) | 832454 |
| Eastern - Central | 1797721 |
| Waterloo and City | 15971 |
| | |
| Special | |
| Western (excluding Waterloo and City Railway) | 919 |
| Eastern - Central | 1082 |
| Waterloo and City | 0 |
| | |
| Empty | |
| Western | 15160 |
| Eastern - Central | 12029 |
| | |
| OTHER MILES | |
| Shunting | 891 |
| | |
| DEPARTMENTAL MILES | 8187 |

**Steam Engine Miles and Hours**

| STEAM ENGINE MILES | MILES | HOURS |
|---|---|---|
| Coaching | | |
| Train | 1979400 | 127386 |
| Shunting | 152733 | 30358 |
| Assisting and light | 102316 | 14799 |
| | | |
| Freight | | |
| Train | 556790 | 60590 |
| Shunting | 526109 | 104891 |
| Assisting and light | 104598 | 11041 |

**Electric Car Miles**

| ELECTRIC CAR MILES | |
|---|---|
| Western (excluding Waterloo and City Railway) | 5033496 |
| Eastern - Central | 9983253 |
| Waterloo and City | 50212 |

*The 1930 station at Sutton Common, then in an oasis of green without the residential development that would follow.*

**Miles run by Sentinel and Petrol Cars**
SENTINEL CAR
Passenger loaded 2213, empty 154, departmental 36
PETROL CARS
Nil
ENGINEERS DEPARTMENT
Nil

**Miles run by Diesel Engines**
5525

**Miles Run by Southampton Dock Engines**
Coaching Shunting          2270
Freight Shunting  25705

**10350    Working of Passenger Trains (Punctuality) FEBRUARY 1938**

**STEAM TRAINS WEEKDAYS**

| DIVISION | No. of trains run | Right time | Average late arrival (mins) |
|---|---|---|---|
| London East | 17758 | 13810 (78%) | 0.81 |
| London Central | 17134 | 10810 (63%) | 1.33 |
| London West | 9624 | 7345 (76%) | 0.71 |
| Isle of Wight | 4252 | 3654 (86%) | 0.31 |
| Southern | 8592 | 7072 (82%) | 0.55 |
| Western | 10351 | 9405 (91%) | 0.33 |
| TOTAL | 67711 | 52106 (77%) | 0.79 |

## STEAM TRAINS SUNDAYS

| DIVISION | No. of trains run | Right time | Average late arrival (mins) |
|---|---|---|---|
| London East | 1320 | 1061 (80%) | 1.04 |
| London Central | 1258 | 845 (67%) | 1.11 |
| London West | 568 | 405 (71%) | 1.35 |
| Isle of Wight | 320 | 295 (92%) | 0.11 |
| Southern | 407 | 331 (81%) | 0.79 |
| Western | 220 | 180 (82%) | 0.46 |
| TOTAL | 4093 | 3117 (76%) | 0.98 |

## ELECTRIC TRAINS WEEKDAYS

| DIVISION | No. of trains run | Right time | Average late arrival (mins) |
|---|---|---|---|
| London East | 40009 | 29580 (74%) | 0.62 |
| London Central | 52385 | 40634 (76%) | 0.53 |
| London West | 31038 | 23013 (74%) | 0.6 |
| TOTAL | 124430 | 93227 (75%) | 0.58 |

## ELECTRIC TRAINS SUNDAYS

| DIVISION | No. of trains run | Right time | Average late arrival (mins) |
|---|---|---|---|
| London East | 4808 | 4299 (89%) | 0.25 |
| London Central | 6174 | 5406 (88%) | 0.25 |
| London West | 3176 | 2877 (91%) | 0.22 |
| TOTAL | 14158 | 12582 (89%) | 0.24 |

Days omitted –

London East Division
February 2. Derailment between Parks Bridge and Hither Green
February 3. Engine failure at Swanley on 6:35a.m. Gillingham to Charing Cross
February 17. Track circuit failure St. Johns, Lewisham and Lee

London Central
February 13. ice on rails between Keymer Junction and Lewes
February 15. ice on rails

London West
February 10. failure of 9:20 p.m. Portsmouth Harbour to Waterloo

## 10351 London and Hastings Train Service.

It was reported that as a result of representations made by the Boroughs of Hastings and Bexhill for improved train services to London, consequent upon the postponement of "Hastings No. 2" Electrification scheme. It has been decided to run one electric train in each direction, Mondays to Fridays inclusive between Hastings and Victoria, calling at St. Leonards (Warrior Square), Bexhill Central, Lewes and East Croydon only, no call being made at Eastbourne.

These services which will be put into force on Monday, the 2 May, will leave Hastings and Victoria at 9.34 a.m. and 7.15 p.m. respectively, and will be for the benefit of residents of Hastings and Bexhill who wish to come up to town for shopping and matinee purposes.

The net increase in loaded train and car miles will be as under,-

Train miles per week       780
Car     "     "     "       4680.

**(To be continued)**

*Fifteen years separate these two views and yet they depict similar workings. Top - A down freight passes South Acton in July 1945 No 3167 hauling two dead WD locos, Nos 75293 and 75294. In the lower view Standard tanks Nos 82012 and 82014 double head the 12.30 pm Fawley to Bevois Park freight through Southampton Central on 31 May 1960 including WD 0-6-0ST No WD106 'Spyck' on its way from the Marchwood Military Railway to Longmoor for overhaul.*

# CARRIAGE CLEANING

*Carriage cleaning facilities at Ramsgate circa 1957 P Ransome-Wallis*

Carriage washing (and internal cleaning) is an unsung yet essential aspect of maintaining the passenger fleet. The date of installation of the first carriage washing facilities on the Southern is not confirmed but it is believed to have been around the 1930s and concurrent with the expansion of electrification. Prior to this, exterior carriage washing had been undertaken by hand, a laborious and time-consuming process also fast becoming ever more costly.

The automatic carriage wash solved this problem at a stroke, the principles of which have also changed little over the years and which are also broadly similar to the automated wash available for motor cars at many garages.

Where the rail and road versions differ is that with the motor vehicle the machine moves back and forth whereas with the rail version it is the washer that remains still and the train that passes through.

Speed is also critical, 3 mph the maximum permitted, but which still allows for a six-coach train to be washed in two minutes. (Any greater speed and the vehicle sides could dislodge the actual brushes - in reality revolving strips of cloth.)

With a locomotive hauled set, an operator was positioned on the ground watching and listening for the driver of the engine to indicate he was clear of the wash and that the equipment might then be turned on. If this assessment was not accurate then the first few feet of the leading vehicle might miss the wash.

Readers may wish to refer to 'Wash & Brush Up' by Pat Kinsella accessible at: http://www.davidheyscollection.com/page30.htm, also the March 1957 issue of 'Railway Magazine'.

*Opposite -* *The wash at Orpington on 13 May 1946 and at which it was reported, "the trains are driven through fairly fast". The water used was drained, filtered and pumped through the system for re-use.*

*Above* - *The double wash at Clapham, note the operator poised on the ground. The notice read, 'Warning to Staff. Speed to be reduced to 3 mph, heads to kept inside engine…..men not to ride on step boards" Although not mentioned, somebody would also be responsible for seeing all windows and droplights were closed.*

*Left -* Clapham Junction 1935.

*Bottom -* The same location, this time in 1949.

*Opposite -* Contemporary facilities at St Leonards West Marina in June 1958.

# 'THE GRID'

## John Burgess

Some months ago, I dug out an old pile of tatty, yellowing Meccano Magazines which I had acquired during my childhood, swapped with a friend for some long forgotten items, maybe a bag of marbles or a stack of cigarette cards. I feel that I probably got the best of the bargain. In October 1952, an anonymous contributor wrote an article entitled "Those Other Named Trains" in which a steam passenger service running between Twickenham and Hampton for the benefit of schoolboys attending Hampton Grammar School is described. For reasons that are now lost in the mists of time, the boys unofficially named the train "The Grid". The article was accompanied by a grainy photograph of an M7 standing at the head of a set of arc-roofed coaches, probably of ex-LB&SCR origin, in the up platform at Hampton station during Southern Railway days. It is impossible to detect a number on the M7 because of the poor quality of the reproduction.

In a discussion forum on the Hampton People's Network, I subsequently discovered a second photograph of M7 No. 25 carrying duty number 157 on a similar set of coaches at the same location. General consensus was that this was also a photograph of "The Grid".

Later still, I stumbled across a contribution from R.E. Tustin (a former pupil at Hampton Grammar School and regular user of "The Grid") in the Railway Magazine for June 1963 hidden away in the regular monthly "Loco Notes", in which he described an occasion when the train was headed by a G16 class 4-8-0T. It appears that nobody had a camera to hand to record this unique appearance, and it set me wondering as to whether this might have been the only occasion when a member of this class hauled a passenger carrying service. It also set me thinking about the possibility of painting the train at a suitably distinctive location on its journey.

My research into this long-forgotten steam service unearthed a surprising amount of detail, much of which must be attributed to the painstaking records kept by R.E. Tustin, no doubt from his schooldays. I have previously come across this railway enthusiast as a modeller from a superb garden railway he produced, which was described and illustrated many years ago in the Model Railway News, with views of "O" gauge Southern Railway locomotives hauling authentic stock through well-constructed rockeries in his garden, all beautifully illustrated with diagrams showing how to produce the right garden setting for a model railway. Enough of this digression.

"The Grid" was unusual in providing a residual steam passenger service in an area that saw most of its services electrified as early as 1915. The train was withdrawn because the school was relocated in 1939 and it was easier to serve the new premises by trolleybus. Steam was retained because a shunting engine was required at Hampton and it suited the Southern Railway to make use of it to haul this school service, rather than allocate an electric unit. It was usual to put an M7 0-4-4T on the service, but over the years Adams Jubilee class 0-4-2s and his earlier large wheeled 4-4-0s were used, as well as Urie H16 class 4-6-2Ts and of course the memorable day when a G16 turned up. As well as running morning and afternoon services, a return trip to Twickenham also ran at lunchtime, leaving Hampton at 12.15 p.m. and arriving back at 1.20 p.m. If the shunting engine was too busy to cover this working, a relief would be dispatched, frequently an Adams 0-4-4T. The steam locomotives were provided by Feltham depot. Stock was either one or two ex-LSWR four-coach block sets, or a three-coach ex-LB&SCR set. The afternoon train left Hampton at 4.14 p.m.

Mr Tustin clearly kept very detailed diaries, because not only does he identify the day when the G16 achieved its starring role (October 2nd 1928), he also recorded the stock (a low-roofed seven-compartment bogie third followed by a standard LSWR 4-coach block set), the number of the locomotive (494), and the fact that the locomotive was running bunker first on its journey to Twickenham, so there was plenty of information to help with a painting.

I decided that I would set the painting on the triangular junction at Strawberry Hill, running along the west to north line with the electric train depot in the background. The only detail I have changed is the orientation of the locomotive which I felt would look much better if it was running chimney first. I apologise if this causes any offence, but I don't think these massive tank engines look particularly attractive from the rear, and I wanted to show it in front of the electric train depot, with the train running towards Twickenham. Although there is some doubt about what the seven-compartment third might be, I think that in all probability it was one of the LSWR's early bogie coaches. These were very short at just 42 feet and they frequently appeared as single vehicles attached to more modern stock right up until their withdrawal in the 1920s and '30s, probably used as strengthening vehicles when demand for extra seats required it. I have got into trouble before with paintings showing locomotives facing in the wrong direction!

A number of the original suburban electric units lurk in the depot sidings. These were converted from LSWR steam stock, and fitted with distinctive torpedo-shaped cabs. Electrification was carried out to provide a means of competing with the trams, which were taking away passengers at an alarming rate and the LSWR third-rail system was perpetuated by the Southern Railway after 1923. On suburban lines, only goods services remained steam-hauled after electrification. The original units lasted into the 1950s until finally being replaced by steel-bodied units.

Strawberry Hill depot was originally built as a steam shed but converted to service electric units after the 1915 electrification. When the G16 class was first introduced, these locomotives were housed at Strawberry Hill for a short time pending completion of the depot at Feltham. No. 494 was based at Feltham when it hauled "The Grid" in 1928. The depot sits in the centre of the triangular junction and the line from Kingston to Shepperton passes from left to right behind the depot. It too is now a rare survivor, an ex-LSWR steam depot still in railway use. The train is approaching the junction with the Kingston to Twickenham line, out of sight to the left of the painting.

Although it is unusual in the 21st century for autumn leaves to appear as early as October 2nd, I certainly remember from my schooldays in the 1960s, that the trees started to turn earlier than they do now and I have given some of the trees a hint of yellow to suggest that summer is coming to an end.

The Magazine article postulates that this unique Southern Railway steam-hauled passenger service was probably the last in the London Area after electrification, and I can't think of any other regularly running over electrified lines, assuming that all main line services and steam-hauled services running out of London such as those on the Oxted lines are discounted. The only remotely similar service would be the one from Clapham Junction to Kensington Olympia which lasted into the 1960s, but over a route not forming part of the old Southern Railway and only carrying a limited passenger service.

### References

*"Those Other Named Trains", unattributed authorship, Meccano Magazine, October 1952*

*"Loco Notes", Railway Magazine, June 1963. Reported by R.E. Tustin*

*Discussion Forum on Hampton People's Network (hamptonpn.ning.com) - Try a search for "M7 0-4-4 Hampton Station" to view what is believed to be a rare photograph of "The Grid"*

*Sister engine, 'G16' No 493 on more normal duties: at Feltham. (Well it fits in with our lead article in this issue as well....) We are well aware that unadvertised 'School' trains ran in a number of other locations, Brockenhurst for example. Further information would be welcome - Ed.*

# ALFRED CARTER 'STATION MASTER'
# Tony Carter

My father, Alf Carter, was born in Dunbridge in 1891 where his father was a signalman. He had wanted to be on the railway since boyhood but had to wait for a clerical vacancy on the London & South Western Railway. In the meantime he took local work until a vacancy arose. Eventually though he was taken on and after an interview and medical, probably at Southampton, he started at his home station at Dunbridge.

In 1909 he was sent to Liss being expected to lodge – as indeed was customary for the time. Here he performed early and late turns and was also involved in parcels and goods charging, reading time tables and the dozens of other duties expected of a booking clerk plus, as might be expected, station accountancy. In addition he was expected to understand (and presumably use) the single needle telegraph, then the accepted means of communication in the same way as a telephone or email might be used today. He also copied documents when necessary, although the technology of the period involved a copying press which appeared to involve pressing pages into a special book and applying pressure after which, somehow, a copy appeared on special paper. I imagine he was happy there and also used his privilege fares to travel home as often as possible.

When the First World War started, he and his brother decided they should do their bit and so enlisted in the army. Alf was sent to Bedford for training and then served in France and Belgium, something he rarely talked about. On returning to railway employment he went as a clerk to Woolston, again going into lodgings. After a few years he applied to go on the relief staff, having also passed his stationmaster's rules and regulations exams. He was then used in either capacity going to small stations such as Corfe Castle, Fordingbridge and also on the Somerset and Dorset line, again having to lodge. This was all within what was then the old Southampton division. After he married he was able to live in a modern semi-detached house at Southampton with a garden, electric light and running water. What luxury!

Promotion for clerical staff wishing to be considered for a station master post was then operated on the simple 'wait to be offered' basis, after which came an interview. If such an offer were rejected then the candidate's name was placed at the bottom of the list. In this way he was successful in obtaining the vacancy at Porton station

*Empty country station with oil lamps and a solitary car. This is Porton between Salisbury and Grateley and the first station where Alf Carter was in permanent charge.*

*The newly rebuilt Seaton Junction looking west. Two platform and two through lines. The Seaton branch platform was at the end of the down platform curving off to the left behind the signal box. The coaches are in the down sidings.*

where the Bulford branch left the Waterloo-West of England route.

At Porton there was everything then associated with a rural location. In the early 1920s, nearly all goods came and were dispatched by rail so the yard would have been busy. This included livestock, fish, milk, mail etc in addition to the smaller items that arrived and departed by train. There was also a delivery vehicle, at the time, probably horse-drawn. The station was lit by oil, as was the house, with water pumped up from outside. One perhaps slightly unusual feature was on the opposite side of the line, where a field was provided for the use of the incumbent station master. Even so, a considerable change from his previous abode, the new house in Southampton.

The family remained at Porton for a few years but in 1933 Dad was offered the post at Seaton Junction. This was a new station recently rebuilt with two through lines and electric light on the platform but still with oil lamps in the station house. The house adjoined the station, the buildings being on the 'up' side including a lovely garden with a gate on to the platform. This station was very busy, especially on summer Saturdays. From here the Seaton branch train departed, having a through coach to and from Waterloo most days. On summer Saturdays the Atlantic Coast Express had a longer portion for Lyme Regis and Seaton, which was worked forward, having been detached at Salisbury. Summer was such a busy time that at weekends an inspector would be present in the signal box to prioritize train running including goods - of which there was a lot. In addition the Express Dairy chose Seaton Junction for its new egg and milk depot, which meant milk was frequently sent away either in churns or in a train of milk tanks to Vauxhall; this was in addition to all the usual parcels and freight.

At Seaton Junction most of the passengers came

off the main line trains but some originated from the nearby villages of Shute or Whitford. The rebuilt station had been provided with a refreshment room on the down side, although logic would have dictated the up side would probably have been better as sometimes people for London had a short wait, whereas those coming off down trains and going to Seaton walked across the platform and immediately joined the branch working. The Seaton coaches were hauled by an 'O2' or 'M7', the vehicles often old LSWR 'gate' stock. Passenger comforts in this stock was not a high priority as the lamp shades might be full of rain water and the lights very dim. To recharge the batteries, the branch train had on occasion to make a trip on the main line, feverishly running up and down between adjacent stations.

With war clouds threatening, another move was on the cards and Alf was appointed Station Master at Petersfield in 1939. Each time we moved, our furniture went by rail in a container and the garden items in a box wagon. Petersfield was the junction for the Midhurst line whilst Dad also supervised Buriton sidings and the level crossings at Petersfield, Kingsfernsden & Sheet. There was then no by-pass for Petersfield and the road crossing was very busy. It could however have been even worse as at least Midhurst branch trains usually used their own separate platform on the London side of the crossing. There was an up loop platform at Petersfield but this was not electrified and so tended to be used only for van trains starting from the station. The regular service comprised two stopping electric trains most hours of the day with an hourly fast service which did not call. The stopping trains were usually 2x 2 BIL units and the fasts 4 COR sets. In the morning and evening one fast train did stop, although its length meant that one end would be off the end of the platform.

Come the black out and blue bulbs were used on the platforms with lights on the trains very dim, even so I do

*Left -* Alf Carter outside his front door at Petersfield.
*Right -* The occasion of a General Manager's visit to Petersfield. Alf is talking to two officials on the down platform, Petersfield signal box and the infamous road crossing are in the background.

not recall any accidents to passengers. During the blitz trains might be turned back at Clapham Junction or Wimbledon and we would occasionally see 'NOL' or 'HAL' units used. Some older engines, such as members of the 'A12' class might also appear on goods trains instead of the more normal 'Q' or '700'. As Portsmouth Harbour station was badly bombed it only had one operational platform and in consequence the only services now using that station were the Waterloo fasts, stopping services terminating at the lower level Portsmouth & Southsea

Some of the trains of war supplies ran via Midhurst, thought to be safer and with the option of being able to shelter in Midhurst tunnel in emergency. Passengers were discouraged from travelling but naval personnel from Portsmouth and soldiers from Longmoor and Bordon (via Liss) used the station frequently in the evenings. I also recall that there was quite a bit of vandalism.

Petersfield station house was a rambling place, very cold with three storeys lit by gas. There was also a cellar which we slept in during air raids. This latter part was

very damp and I can still smell the coal, oil, vegetables etc which were stored there. There was a connecting door from the house to the SM's office. As in 1914, some railway staff joined HM forces although a lot were exempt. Including shunters, signalmen, platform and goods staff, the total at Petersfield would be about 40, ranging in age from 14 to 70 or even over and including several women. The 'lamp boy' would clean and refill all the signal lamps and of necessity walk alongside the electrified lines through Buriton tunnel. With what spare time they had, the staff spent their hours either with the fire service, police, home-guard or as an air-raid warden, somehow also finding time to cultivate their allotment gardens and grow their own vegetables. There was only a small back garden with the station house but there was an enormous garden on the other side of the 'up' side coal yard. Unfortunately being out of sight, a lot of produce simply disappeared either by public trespassers or possibly engine drivers.

As mentioned earlier, if you were offered promotion you were expected to move, it being considered

*Sittingbourne with a train for the Kent coast just leaving. Three platform faces and, at the time, an overall-roof and of course no electrification.*

bad manners to refuse, with your name then going to the bottom of the list. But when Alf was offered the post at Portland he did refuse on the basis the station had been blitzed and a number of the staff killed. Instead, in 1944, he was offered promotion to the post of SM at Sittingbourne, not an area we knew at all. Here was also a location affected by the enemy, for the main line had recently been severed when a 'doodle bug' dived under a local bridge as a train was passing over. Kent was clearly not a safe place to live. Even so he took the post

Sittingbourne was the junction for Sheerness, then the busiest branch line on the SR. There were HM dockyards at Chatham and Sheerness and a mine sweeper base at Queenborough. Freight traffic was also very heavy especially to and from the branch plus Ridham Dock, between Kemsley and Queenborough. Shunting at Sittingbourne went on 24/7, five shunters dealing with agriculture, livestock, milk, mails, plus wartime requirements and small items for local delivery. The latter was undertaken by a fleet of three horse-drawn carts and a motor vehicle. There were in the order of 50 staff.

The train service was steam worked, London trains usually hauled by a 'King Arthur' or 'Schools' or, much later a 'West Country'. Local trains between Faversham and Chatham might have an 'E1' or 'D1' in charge, the branch

services usually behind an 'H' or 'R1', this engine running round its train at each end, with the platform porters uncoupling and coupling. The service was irregular, an example being that there were two Cannon Street trains morning and evening but the first train to Victoria was at 9.5am. On Sundays there was a train every 2 or 3 hours. The station also closed briefly at lunch time.

The station house was lit by gas: it made a change from oil! The three platforms had a felt roof on the canopies, meaning the view from the house upstairs was non-existent, as all one could see was the slope of the roof. I recall my first job was to black out all the windows of the house, an enormous task.

Dad had five signal boxes under him, Sittingbourne 'A' & 'B', Western and Middle Junction on the Sheerness triangle and Kemsley Halt where trains crossed on the single line. In addition he controlled three private sidings, special instructions being issued for engines to turn on the triangle when servicing the siding near Western Junction. In the summer, Sittingbourne ran special trains of fruit to London markets, extra staff being needed. For the cherry season it was not unknown to send off 200 tons a fruit in a single day.

The station house here was grim. There was only a kitchen and scullery downstairs with a toilet across the back yard, all other rooms leading off a long corridor upstairs.

After blacking out the windows, the next task was laying linoleum in each room before placing furniture. This was a station master post not many would have welcomed, not assisted by the fact it was hard to obtain suitable staff in consequence of factory competition offering better wages and better hours.

People have asked what were the duties of a station master? In reality this varied from station to station and depended on how many staff and how experienced they were. It could also be subdivided into operating, commercial and general. To take the last first, cleaning, lighting, heating, station repairs, correct display of publicity, supply of uniforms and protective clothing and 'generally good housekeeping'. Next we might refer to the term 'Commercial'. This would be the banking of cash, paying wages and checking accounts, the latter done daily, weekly and monthly. There was also responsibility for dealing with ticket irregularities, barrier efficiency, meeting claims for damage, public enquiries and complaints and much more. Finally 'Operating'. This was ensuring safety regulations were observed by signalmen and shunters and putting in appearances outside normal hours to do so, ensuring signal boxes were in circuit to deal with engineering requirements and that staff knew what to do in an emergency. Some stations might also have special local requirements e.g. if a lifting bridge was in their patch or possibly cleaning sheds.

Perhaps fortunately, after about five years at Sittingbourne Alf was offered promotion to SM at Worthing Central which included West Worthing and Durrington. There was a goods agent at Worthing who dealt with the commercial side of things but because there were only two shunters based there clearly the Goods Agent was at the wrong station! There were electric cleaning sheds at West Worthing which was also Alf's first experience having guards and carriage cleaners under him. Worthing Central, as is was then, and West Worthing both frequently sent garden produce to London markets but when Dad was told what an enormous undertaking it was, he laughed. After Sittingbourne it was trivial.

Worthing was also the first place where station accommodation was not provided. As a result he lodged for a while, that is until British Railways, as it had then become, bought a house for the SMs use. They chose a terrace property house about 1½ miles from the station and had to provide a telephone but at least here was electric light and a garden, albeit very small by station house standards.

Alf remained at Worthing until retirement. He clearly liked the place and, as he recalled, there were good staff helped by having less competition or work outside. He enjoyed his railway career and sometimes gave talks about it. Following retirement he remained in Worthing and for a short time acted as a custodian at nearby Arundel Castle.

*Alf's final railway posting, Worthing Central. As with Sittingbourne, three platforms but this time electrified lines.*

# MOMENTS

*Above* - Rummaging through the archives, and........LSWR 'F13' 4-6-0 No 330 passing Kennington Junction signal box south of Oxford with the 10.15 am Leamington to Eastleigh coal train.
*Bottom* - SECR No 16 at Caterham on the 9.39 am to Charing Cross.

Another 'bumper-bundle' (that phrase is showing my age) of comments and feedback on previous issues of 'SW'. We start with Stephen Grant: "I can add a couple of footnotes to Mike King's description of the Southern's bullion vans (Variations on Luggage Vans Part 2, SW 26).

"When I was a junior clerk in Woking and Southampton Controls (1964-7), special trains would periodically operate from Southampton Docks to Waterloo carrying gold bullion for the Bank of England. These would consist of a steam locomotive (typically an Eastleigh 76xxx Mogul or whatever else was available on the day), three or four bullion vans and a passenger vehicle (typically a BR Standard corridor brake second) to accommodate the guard and about 20 uniformed policemen. There was no particular secret about the purpose and contents of the train, at least not among the signalmen, station staff and control staff involved in their working. From memory, the Special Notice for these workings used the telegraphic codeword 'SPECIE'.

"I left BR in 1967 to join Union Castle Line, whose ships on the Cape mail route were fitted with a secure 'specie room' for transporting bars of gold bullion from the South African goldmines. Here I was able to get a closer look at the bullion vans on those occasions when they were positioned on the quay adjacent to 102 berth in Southampton Western Docks ready to receive an incoming consignment. As Mike says, they had no markings to draw attention to themselves apart from "RETURN TO SOUTHAMPTON DOCKS" or something similar and at first sight they looked just like any other rather grubby green PMV. It was only when the outer doors were opened that one saw that they were strong-rooms on wheels. It would certainly make for an interesting special working on a model railway!"

*This page and opposite - Images from the 'Hampshire Hog' railtour.. Above 'M7' No 30667, right hand column: 'Q1' No 33035 at Bordon, and opposite the cover of the tour brochure and waiting at Hampstead Norris. Photographs by Geoff Bird.*

Now from Geoff Bird. "I have just been reading SW No. 24 (yes - I am a little bit behind the times as I now have retired and live abroad - buy SW once a year) and was very interested to read the article about the "Hampshire Hog" railtour.

"At that time (14 March 1964), I was still a schoolboy and living with my parents at Epsom. I had been on a few railtours before but was interested in this one because of the motive power offered as well as the route. I think that passenger services over the DN&S had been withdrawn by that time (Ed - yes they had) and the 'Alps' line was being operated by the SR DEMUs.

"Unfortunately the tour was not blessed with the best of luck with the weather or with the motive power. I travelled by train from Epsom to Guildford where the tour engine, M7 30667, was in the shed yard while I awaited a train to Ash, where the trip was to start. Unfortunately, I did not take a photo even though the weather at that time was good. No 30667 was a Bournemouth-based loco and had obviously made a long trip (presumably via Eastleigh and Alton) to get to Guildford. Interestingly enough, it was actually No. 30106, having taken over the number 30667 when it was p-p fitted in 1961 and the original 30667 was then scrapped. It was finally withdrawn a couple of months later in May 1964, although whether it saw any more active service after our trip is debatable.

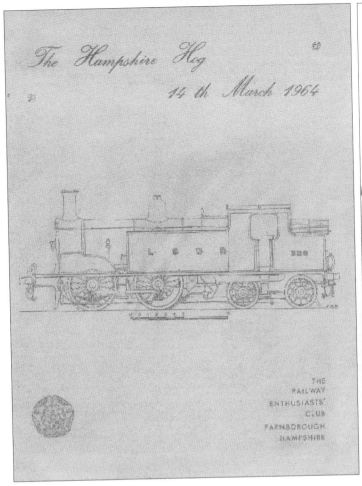

"It was pouring with rain, however, by the time the loco arrived at Ash together with p-p set No. 610 (including headboard) on time, but we then sat there without moving. It was finally announced that the loco had failed and that an alternative would be provided as soon as possible. This turned out to be Q1 class No. 33035, not of course push-pull fitted. We finally left Ash at 10.30 am with our first to the Bordon branch where the Q1 was able to run round its train. We had been scheduled to traverse the remnants of the Meon Valley to Farringdon and the Basingstoke branch from Alton as far as Treloar's siding but this was now impossible without a push-pull fitted loco whilst in addition we were also very far behind time. Instead, after returning off the Bordon line to Bentley and again running round, we continued from Alton directly to Eastleigh where we had been promised another M7 would be waiting to take the train on the next stage of our journey. However, when we arrived at Eastleigh (still in pouring rain) it transpired that Ivatt 2MT No. 41329 would be the loco to take us over the DN&S to Didcot. Not even having time to have a look around the shed at Eastleigh, we set off for Didcot. By 3.30 pm we had reached Whitchurch where a stop was made for the loco to take water and to pass a diesel hauled southbound freight. We also had a photographic stop, as planned, at Hampstead Norris. By

now it had more or less stopped raining, so this is where I managed to get a couple of photos including the one of the headboard, still mounted on the front of the p-p set - but by now the back of the train - hence the tail-light. When we reached Didcot, the 2MT went to shed for servicing and we were able to have a look around what was later to become the GWS Headquarters. At that time there were quite a few locomotives stored outside including 43xx class 2-6-0s Nos. 5330 and 6385 and 2251 class No. 2221. Hall class No. 5936 'Oakley Hall' was outside in the shed yard. By this time the light was failing rapidly so the photographs are not very good.

"My recollections of the journey are very hazy - it had been a long day by then. I assume that we travelled back along the GW main line to Reading, gaining SR territory again as I seem to recollect that the train terminated at Ascot, although I cannot be sure of this. All I can remember is managing to get back to Guildford in time to catch the last train back to Epsom and home. By now the time was almost midnight and my parents were starting to get worried (being only 16 at the time). I though had been on several railtours before and they knew what to expect in terms of timekeeping of such enterprises.
Please pass on my good wishes to Ron Mason for a very interesting article". *(We have indeed done this - Ed.)*

Geoff forwarded a second piece shortly afterwards with some more information, "When one looks at the timings, there are a few corrections to my original recalled points. Firstly, the train had started from Farnborough North, although I joined it at Ash. Because of the delay in getting a replacement loco, departure time was not until 10.08 am instead of the scheduled 9.17 am. - probably not bad when one thinks that they had to contact Guildford shed and get a spare loco to the train at Ash. We were still about 30 minutes down returning to Bentley from the Bordon branch but by missing out the branch lines from Alton we were slightly ahead of time at Alton and fully on schedule at Medstead & Four Marks. The original plan had been to make an unusual manoeuvre at Shawford Junction, the M7 booked to stop on the down main and then reverse back on to the DNS before running down the relief from Shawford Junction and the back of Shawford station. Again, the lack of a push-pull fitted loco precluded this and instead we continued straight down the main to Eastleigh to arrive at 1.25 pm  Here a new loco was put on the front very promptly (No 41329) and we left again at 1.33 pm  Obviously, the 2MT did us proud because we were through Newbury and arrived at our booked photo stop at Hampstead Norris ahead of time at 3.20 p.m.  Arrival at Didcot was also slightly ahead of time at 4.29 pm (it was getting dark by then on what was a murky March afternoon) and left again 12 minutes late at 5.18 pm  From there, we were more or less on time through to Ascot although it was after that when the delays started.  According to my notes, we spent 25 minutes at Virginia Water followed by another 25 minute wait at Staines before going through Virginia Water again at 8.18 pm. Thus Addlestone Junction was reached at 8.26 p.m. instead of 6.56 pm (one and a half hours late) and Woking at 8.44 pm.  This is where I left the train to continue to Guildford, although I did note that whilst I waiting the special train left for its final destination of 'Farnborough Main' at 8.50 pm. I have no recollection of why we went to Staines and then back to Virginia Water, I can only think it had something to do with the availability of water."

Now continuing on our theme of Britannias – see 'Rebuilt' in No 27 - a bit more from Mr U W R Casebourbe, "I have just read the rebuilt section of SW25 with a request for information on the Braitannias working boat trains via Chatham. I lived in Canterbury then near Bekesbourne 1950 -65 and saw No 70004 on the down 'Arrow' at Canterbury on several Sundays in the 1950s due to Sunday diversions. I also once saw No 70014 on the 9.20 am Dover Priory to Victoria at Bekesbourne – the only up goods train from Canterbury to Victoria weekdays - a heavy train which produced 'MNs', 'Light Pacifics', 'Arthurs', 'Schools', 73xxx and 75xxx types and once even an 'N'.

"Incidentally it is perhaps not generally known that even after the Chatham electrification in June 1959 there continued to be a steam boat train via Chatham Hill until June 1961: the 9.30 am Victoria to Dover Marine and 5.25 pm ex-Dover Marine. The 'Night Ferry' booked to be CL71xxx hauled on this route, was occasionally steam-hauled after June 1959 during adverse winter weather. Occasionally specials went this way with steam after 1959. e.g.; hockey specials to Wembley on 11 March 1961 with No 34089 and No 34073.

Kevin Dakin adds reference Britannias, "Don't forget No 70000 was seen passing through Fratton en route to London with a special, the LCGB 'The Vectis Rail Tour on 4 October 1964."

This from Adrian Westbury referring to No 26. "Another enjoyable issue of SW with a good cross section of topics.

"I was fortunate to pick up a copy of your preview issue when it was published and have obtained a copy of each issue since. Two items in No 26 that I would like to share my comments with you. The photo on page 4 of the condemned 4-SUB, I wouldn't think it was left there too long as the second and third vehicles appear to be Bulleid stock that used to augment (Southern term) trains from 3 to 4 car and then of course were reused in new 4-SUB units, hence they would be unlikely to be left to deteriorate very long.

"The photo by Mr Townroe of the diesel shunter receiving attention in the open air brought back memories to me. I served a five-year engineering apprenticeship with British Railways, the first three years of which were at Brighton works - where I commenced at the same time as Brian Potts (who penned two articles on the works in early issues of SW) and the final two years at Stourbridge MPD on the Western Region. Towards the end of my time I was detailed to give a diesel shunter of the 13xxx series its monthly service and examination and being a fine late spring / early summer day, asked for it to be positioned outside the shed over a pit road - BIG MISTAKE. After opening the doors and sliding the roof back like the one in the photograph, I removed the injectors and took them to our small workshop to strip, clean and recalibrate. By the time I climbed back on to the loco to refit them and carry on with the service everything was burning hot!  I got both a too warm bum and burnt fingers, much to the amusement of Les the fitter who I worked with and his mate Tom. Such are memories."

From David Morgan, "Thanks for another interesting edition of Southern Way. The photos on page 58 are, as suggested, at Hither Green Down Yard and the original Dover Ferry Sidings. With regard to the lack of a barrier wagon on the tank cars being shunted, the product conveyed will have been heavy fuel oil for the train ferry rather than the more flammable 'class A' products such as petroleum spirit which be more likely to require barrier wagons."

Next from John Raggett, "I have been enjoying once again the latest (26th) issue of the Southern Way. As always, an excellent read. In your editorial, you ask the question, 'So where do we go from here?' ...' is it what the readership wants?' You go on to say it's over to us to 'Tell me what it is you would like to see.' Well, quite frankly, I think you have pitched Southern Way just about right. And this view is shared by other readers that I have talked to. You're right, there is only so much you can say on 'Bulleid / Clapham Junction / signal boxes etc.' but there are a whole wealth of anecdotes to be captured still out there. For example, the recent stories from Bill Trigg, full of interest and sharing with others his experiences of working on the railway (- *more from Bill Trigg will appear in due course - Ed.)* When I left school in 1965 and started work on the railway, I quickly discovered there is a lot more to railways than just trains. Railways are also about people, those that work on them and the, er, customers, as we call them today. (And not just the passengers, those that used to send their goods by rail as well.) Ha ha, I could tell you some stories, ho ho. (Maybe I should write a book, eh?) *(I am waiting....Ed).*

"No, I think you have got things just as people like it. Only one area that could be of benefit for the future, again a view shared by those I have talked to, is to perhaps extend the time line to more recent years. Even the corporate British Rail blue era of the late 60s and throughout the 70s could not sweep away the 'Southern Way' of doing things. I went to Hoo Junction in 1992, just prior to re-organisation in the first step to privatising the railways, and although united as part of the Southern since 1923, there was still a different culture down on the South Eastern to what I was used to. I joked with my colleagues there one day that I had been given the job there as it had needed a South Western man to show them the proper way of doing things! It did indeed take privatisation to wipe out once and for all traditions and identities with the past, so there is scope to broaden the appeal of 'The Southern Way' without breaking too far from the original remit of covering the period up to 1970. After all, even the British Rail blue era is now history, although whether it has quite the same appeal as all things Southern, I'm not sure. There is certainly a lot of enthusiasm for blue diesels! However, one thing doesn't change, and that is the people who work on the railway and its customers who make the stories that brings the past alive."

I replied as follows, "Dear John, Thank you – sincerely. Yours is the only response I have had to my 'flying a kite' so to speak and I do welcome it. Yes of course it is gratifying to know 'SW' is pitched about where it should be but it is also very useful to know of the interest in the post 1970 years.

"The trouble with any regular periodical is it is all too easy to remain stuck in the areas of the editor's personal interest. I have genuinely tried not to do this, indeed I have learnt a lot from reading the submissions made. We all like to think we are railway experts but to set up as such is a dangerous concept from which it is all too easy to be displaced. Expertise in one area, yes, but not every aspect.

"There is also a wealth of difference between having been a professional railwayman (regardless of grade / role / position) and not. I have never been in the former category although as I make my living out of railway books I do hope I may class myself as a 'professional amateur'!

"I take on board your comments. 1970 is in fact fast approaching 50 years past, I think we all look back to what we were doing in the decade so perhaps the time has indeed come for change.

"I will include your letter (intact) in the next issue where there is space. This will have to be in a few months as No 27 is already at the maximum 120 sides. But I do appreciate your comments.

"What I will say is that change has to be gradual – but watch this space. Best wishes etc etc."

Not deliberately connected with the above but there is certainly some continuity with the below from Nicolas Owen, "Good some electric tales in the latest Southern Way. Particularly fascinating was the Chessington branch story. The Zoo mentioned is now called Chessington World of Adventures, and very popular it is. The never-completed rail extension could have included a station opposite World of Adventures. And undoubtedly many folk would have travelled to it by train, since congestion on the approaches in the summer is considerable.

"Now, the redoubtable Chris Green has told that when he was in charge of Network South East, the possibility of such a half-mile extension was examined carefully - but the financial case could not be made. Perhaps a different decision could be reached in these very different, expansion-minded days?" And of course speaking of electrics, I do hope those who follow such things will note the coverage of 2-BILS in No 27......

We continue with some notes about SW26 and another of our recent titles, 'Southern Wagons in Colour', this from Neil Knowlden, "Firstly, Bagnall Works No. 2848 was actually the last of a batch of four metre-gauge 0-6-0 pannier tanks supplied to the Eti Bank Steel Co. in Turkey in 1947 ..... what is shown on page 16 is 'Kent Electric Power Company No. 2' or Bagnall No. 2842 of 1946. This was supplied new to Littlebrook Power Station near Dartford and transferred to 'Croydon A' station in November 1959. The Peckett, on the other hand, was the second of a pair that always worked at 'Croydon B' on the other side of the Wimbledon-West Croydon line (known nowadays as 'IKEA' and 'Tramlink' respectively).

"About 1972, No.2 was 'discovered' by a small band of schoolboys who had 'got the preservation bug' but had been unable to buy a Southern brakevan - in which to display a few enamel signs - as none was available. Contact was made with the CEGB but we were told that the loco was not for sale ...... until that is a Tender Form appeared within a few weeks. By now we were on the verge of becoming impoverished students (higher education) but we counted our pennies and submitted a 'silly' bid - which, to our great surprise, was accepted.

"Both the Bluebell and Kent & East Sussex Railways had grown out of their 'little engine' beginnings so were not interested in providing us a home - but we heard of a scheme about to get underway down in Hampshire and after shunting the loco across to 'B' station, No. 2 left by road to become the first loco at what became the Mid-Hants Railway in 1973. It wasn't long before 'bigger and better' main line locos arrived so the engine languished in various sidings until railway politics triggered a move to the Avon Valley Railway (Bristol) in 1986 - with 'bigger and better' locos and other stock that our group had acquired in the meantime. Though one-time Somerset & Dorset 4F No. 44123 and a couple of goods vans are still at Bitton, the rest of our collection has since been dispersed with No. 2 heading north to the spiritual home of Bagnalls on the Foxfield Railway - where she eventually returned to steam (in somewhat modified form) in 2010. (Attached photos from 1972, 1973, 1974, 1986 & 2010.)

"The Two Pecketts from 'Croydon B' went to Quainton Road about the same time as No. 2 went to Alresford ..... unfortunately, neither the two diesels from 'B' nor the 1925 English Electric electric loco from 'A' made it into preservation - the latter probably of the greatest historic interest of the lot.

"Secondly, page 36 illustrates Bridge No. 476 ( Catford Loop series ) / 672 ( Mid-Kent Line series ) where the two railways cross. I don't think this bridge has changed significantly since the photo was taken and I've long wondered why there appears to be adequate width for three tracks between the abutments here. Might there have been plans for some sort of flying / burrowing junction at one time : As you can see, the Mid-Kent is straight and laid centrally, while there are steel uprights blocking the half-

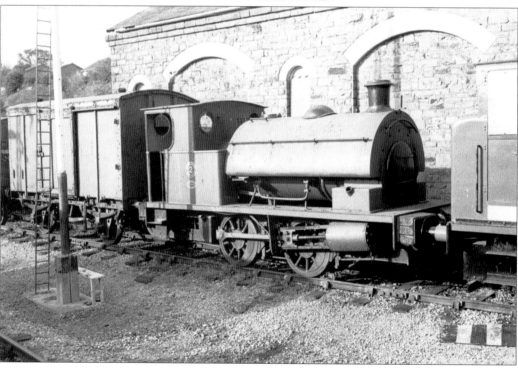

*Neil Knowldens' views No 2 from 1973 (above) and 1986 (left).*

spaces either side so installation of a third track would not be straightforward. (Incidentally, it is gratifying that the Ten -Car Scheme described on these pages was actually implemented - I dread to think how many zillions of pounds were wasted on extending all those platforms for twelve cars that never materialised a few years ago - probably a few decades by now! )

"......... Thirdly - sorry - I don't think the 'motley collection' of stock on page 4 is actually very mottled. The second and third coaches are both Bulleid 'augmentation' stock (rather indistinct beyond there) and it was very rare to see two of these in one augmented set. I reckon, therefore, that the motor coaches from set 4348 have been borrowed as barriers to a whole train of Bulleid trailers waiting to be incorporated in new 4-EPB sets.

"fourthly - p17 : 47203 is NOT a 'Jinty' class 3F ......... the term 'Jinty' has become attached to the LMS Standard 3F Tank but is, in no way, an official class designation - but this isn't an LMS Standard 3F Tank anyway, it's the earlier Midland Railway version.

"fifthly - p58 : I'm pretty sure you've got both locations right ...... 71.011 is actually NOT looking towards the future - other than in terms of its replacement by class 73s - as it was among the majority of the class that went for scrap without rebuilding to class 74 Electro-Diesels (prior to TOPS numbering). 30084 is not in great danger of igniting those tank wagons as they are for 'Class B' traffic ( I bet it was fuel for the ferry.) ...... if they were silver-painted 'Class A' tanks it might be a different matter.

"sixthly - p86 : Mike King advises that 'Bulleid livery changes had so far been largely missed by the non-passenger stock' ......... while the evidence - or rather lack of evidence to the contrary - would seem to support the continued use of obsolete paint into and through the war years it cannot be explained by 'using up old stocks' .... unless the paint buyer had over-ordered by quite a few thousand gallons!"

*(We might add that David Morgan amongst others also kindly contacted us over the issue of fuel being 'Class B' rather than 'Class 1'. Thanks to all for their efforts on this one - Ed.)*

Richard Bell adds his memories of a certain announcer, "A memory has come back to me which is apposite to the second item about trains to Maidstone West. In the 1950s there was an announcer at London Bridge who had his own party trick. "Reer faw coachis fer Cuxtonallinsnodlannooiveaywsferdmaystnbariksanmaystn WES" - awlinwunbref! *(Think some of us may need an interpreter on this one Richard - Ed.)*

From Alan Postlethwaite, "Tunes of Glory. I too have a selection of tunes permanently associated in my mind with railways: The Shadows' 'Apache' - in the bar of a B&B pub at Cranleigh during a two-day walk of the branch line. Cilla Black's 'You're My World' - while exploring the Deal line shortly after electrification. Helen Shapiro's 'Walking Back to Happiness' - while photographing Black

Fives on the Stafford - Wolverhampton line during the Great Freeze of 1962. I remember too the chilblains and the warmth of a Midland Red bus. The Beatles' 'She Loves You, Yeah, Yeah, Yeah' - while commuting to Holborn Viaduct and walking up through Smithfield Market to Northampton College. The meat porters thought I was nuts. Sergei Rachmaninov's 'Piano Concerto No. 2' - every time I see a Stanier 2-6-4 tank, especially with Celia Johnson leaning out of a carriage window with a tear in her eye or when I run her local train on my model railway - the 'Brief Encounter Special'. The Seekers' 'Island of Dreams' - while researching station architecture in the Denmark Hill - Dulwich - Herne Hill - Crystal Palace area. Vivian Ellis' 'Coronation Scot' - every time I see a streamlined LMS Pacific."

Now from Roger MacDonald, "With reference to the picture of Ryde and Billinton Set No. 498 on pp 44-45 of SW Issue No. 26, the same picture but taken from a different angle appears in Maycock and Reed's 'Isle of Wight Steam Passenger Stock', Oakwood Press, stating that it was indeed taken on the Bembridge branch in about October 1929.

Readers may be interested to know that Brake Third 4115 shown in the photograph is currently under restoration in the Carriage and Wagon workshop at Havenstreet on the Isle of Wight Steam Railway and has a projected completion date of about two years' time. Billinton Third 2343 from set 497 has already been restored and has run in traffic for a number of years."

This from John Morgan, "Just obtained copy of Issue No. 26 - great stuff as usual, BUT, front cover picture is I think unit 4586, but it is definitely a Central Section train, Victoria to Epsom via Mitcham Junction - in those days it would have been my train home to Cheam!"

Now the turn of Greg Beecroft. "The interesting article on Southern Coal mentions the ropeway from Tilmanstone Colliery to Dover Harbour. This was a remarkable piece of equipment, so you might be interested in further details, which come from 'The Industrial Eden' (ISBN 0 9515654 0 0) by Richard Tilden Sherren, the grandson of Richard Tilden Smith, who owned the colliery.

"The ropeway was built in order to transport coal to Dover Harbour more cheaply than by train. The SECR and East Kent Light Railway charged 5s 9d per ton from Tilmanstone to Dover, but when the ropeway was in operation Tilden Smith could transport coal at a cost of 1s 9d per ton. The ropeway was proposed in 1909, but the first section did not come into use until 12 October 1929 and the full length on 14 February 1930. It cost £120,000. Sadly, Tilden Smith died in December 1929, so did not see the ropeway completed.

"A Parliamentary Order was required in order to construct the ropeway and this was obtained with some difficulty, particularly because of opposition from the Southern Railway and the EKLR. In response to its construction, they revised their charges for carrying coal from Tilmanstone to Dover to 2s 0d per ton, a 65% reduction.

As completed, the ropeway was 7½ miles long and was supported on 177 pylons or trestles. It approached Dover Harbour through a tunnel, emerging from a portal in the white cliffs, to terminate at a large bunker on the eastern arm. Coal was carried in buckets that could hold 14.5 cwt and the system was said to have the capacity to transport 750,000 tons of coal per year, though that was never achieved. Tilden Smith had a grand vision for a network of ropeways serving a variety of industrial plants, all fed by Tilmanstone coal. These would have included a steel works, cement works, power station and chemical plant. Fortunately for lovers of the Kent countryside, none of these was built.

The Second World War brought coal exports to an end and the ropeway was disused. It fell into disrepair and was dismantled in 1954."

Some very interesting feedback now from C Sayers -Leavy both on 'SW' and also the recent Special issue No 10 featuring material from S C Townroe, "Being a regular collector of the SW series of publications, I missed the start, but have now managed to get a full set of the books right from the Preview issue including all of the 'special' issues to date, I find them very interesting.

"I'm a recently retired Engineer from 37 years in the rail industry (and 8 years in rail preservation before that – starting on the ill-fated Westerham line scheme) and have always been based in Kent, although the only region I didn't work on was the ScR. For the last 30 years I have lived and travelled out from Broadstairs on the Isle of Thanet and my job as a Plant Engineer took me all over the UK.

I have not had the time to comment on your publications before but recently there have been a couple of matters that have brought 'push to shove' so to speak. Please note that any comments that I make are intended to be constructive and are not to be seen in any way as criticisms.

The first matter relates to the article on the Bulleid Double Decker trains. I well remember seeing these in service but I never had the opportunity to ride on them. My comments relate to the caption notes for the picture at the top of page 73 in SW25. I think that this caption and the comment with regard to the standing passengers in particular is an incorrect interpretation of what can be seen in the picture. There is no doubt about the unpopularity of travelling on the 'top deck', which was really a feature of the busy period services inward to London in the morning rush and outward during the evening. We don't appear to have a time of day for the picture ? but I would venture to suggest that it is an 'off or end of peak' service (particularly as there are no other trains to be seen). Now, I have always been surprised by the numbers of passengers that make the short journey between Cannon Street / Waterloo / Charing Cross and London Bridge. The reason for this is of course that a number of mainline services do not call at London

Bridge on the way in + those arriving at Waterloo mainline for the City of London (but not necessarily going to 'Bank') and vice versa for the City of Westminster or just because their work was in the Borough area. Lots of passengers could be seen making these short interconnecting journeys (and this still happens today but to a lesser extent since the 'new technology' changes in the Banking / Insurance business) and very often these people do not even bother to take a seat, particularly if they boarded just as the service was leaving. So I would venture to suggest that this is the reason for the standing passengers seen in the picture, that they will shortly be arriving at London Bridge and they are ready to get off the service and not that they didn't want to venture upstairs.. There was a time when Cannon Street was virtually shut down during the day, the mainline services being a feature of the 'peak' periods only. However, even during this 'shut down' there would still be a shuttle service running to and from London Bridge – just for the purpose of the interchange facility.

"There is also no doubt that the en-train / de-train loading was a problem during the busy periods, none more so than at London Bridge where short platform occupancy was a key feature of maintaining the very intensive services. Indeed the SE&CR knew this only too well when they built their 100 seater coaches, two examples of which survive on the Bluebell Railway. These coaches and the other high density stock that came after them, with a door at every seat bay were the quickest and most efficient way of getting passengers on / off of the services. Ever since this type of stock was withdrawn, getting people on / off the trains has been a growing problem, particularly at London Bridge (as an intermediate rather than terminal stop). I well recall making comments, firstly on the introduction of the Networker stock and subsequently the Javelin, with regard to their limited door openings and their effect on getting people on and off the trains quickly – all to no avail and what do we see today? Take a look at Platform 6 at London Bridge in the busy periods and perhaps Ashford (for the Javelin services) where there is a jam and a crowd of people trying to get on / off the services. It is also only fair to say that the change in the construction of the trains has made this matter worse. Monocoque (stressed skin and no separate underframe) construction does not lend itself to having a bodyside opening 'at every seat bay' and of course this is a 'trade off' for greater body strength, crush and telescoping resistance . One is left wondering if Bulleid pursued the DD design in the face of the loading / gauge problems, because it was a relatively cheap solution? The Southern was of course well known for this sort of approach to its rolling stock engineering problems.

"The second matter also relates to picture captions, this time in the special issue No 10 'S.C. Townrowe's Journey in Steam'. This is another very interesting volume. I had hoped to find more pictures of some of the incidents that he was involved with but perhaps some more of these will appear elsewhere at some future date? *(Many appeared in 'Special Issue No 8 dealing with Accidents etc - Ed.)*

"Firstly, the picture at the top of page 70. This illustration speaks volumes to an engineer !!! I find this a very curious failure and you are right to say that we are left to ponder the cause. This failure may have been the precursor of the other motion failures that occurred in the same incident. Your comment on the number of failures around this time is also very interesting. The buckled coupling rods in the lower picture appear to have failed 'mid span' suggesting some form of 'lock up' at speed occurred. What is very clear from the top picture is the very poor state of the material that the rod is made from. Are there any other pictures available of this incident? I am no expert on the various SR engine types / rebuilding features, but it would appear from checking some of your other published pictures, that, prior to rebuilding, all of the Bulleid Pacific's had 'fluted' coupling rods and that when rebuilt, the Merchant Navy's (only) seem to have been fitted with plain coupling rods along with the Walschaerts valve gear. On page 17 of the same book, you comment on 35018 being the first Merchant Navy to be rebuilt between Nov. 1955 & Feb 1956 – does this mean that the date of the picture / failure on page 70 is wrong ? or was 35016 fitted with plain coupling rods prior to the rebuilding ? I have always been impressed by the quality of the welding on the Bulleid all steel boilers (I worked on the initial restoration of *Blackmore Vale*) and this high level of 'quality control' appeared to be the norm for a main works like Eastleigh's output. However if we return to the failed coupling rod, it is a very different story......This failure is not a fatigue failure and indeed the ultimate failure has not been caused by abnormal (other failure) loadings. The failure cross section reveals very curious strata. There appears to have been an 'inclusion' in the material prior to (or during) its manufacturing into a coupling rod. The dark area of material is entrapped slag (or similar) and the bright areas only would have any strength approx. 50% of the CSA prior to their ultimate failing. Also very curious is the apparent thin 'skin' sections around the outside of the broken end. Traditionally motion rods are hot forged and then machined from solid material, however this is time and energy consuming and another process would be to flash Butt-weld the bearing bosses on to plain 'cut' slab material. Do we know how Eastleigh made these rods ? We do know that after the war there was a lot of poor quality steel in circulation – but with the high level of quality in manufacturing/inspection (as referred to above) one would have thought that any poor material would have been identified during manufacturing and indeed the pre manufacturing material inspection processes......

"And now a few comments on the recovery of 30477, particularly as you say that 'SCT' did not elaborate on matters when discussing his pictures. The picture at the top of page 77 is a little more than just 'stabilising' the engine – although 'in summary' this is a correct description. The picture illustrates the use of the German MFD hydraulic re-railing equipment. This system was truly hydraulic in its

*'Lest we forget' - indeed. Railway Staff Memorial, Gillingham Kent, c1938.*     *Tony Andrews*

literal sense – as it actually used water as the pressure medium, mixed with soluble oil (similar to cutting fluid used in machine shops). The two long rams are part of the equipment that was available for 'righting' or even 'raising' vehicles back to their correct orientation i.e. standing on their wheels. The 'chains around the boiler' are not taking any load in this operation – they are just the loose ends, that are tied off on the LHS hand rails to stop them dropping back down. It is the other end of the chains that are taking the load. Attaching this relatively new equipment to a steam loco that would not have any purpose designed jacking points (as per modern traction equipment) – could be quite fraught and likely to cause further damage to the engine and

**CONDUCTED DAY TOUR BY ALL-PULLMAN TRAIN
WITH OBSERVATION CAR TO**

# SALISBURY & WINCHESTER

Delightful Coach Tour of Salisbury and Stonehenge, with
Conducted Tour of the famous cathedral city of Winchester

## WEDNESDAY, 17TH AUGUST

### ALL - IN - FARES

(Rail Journey, Coach Trip, Luncheon and Tea
on Train)

| 1st CLASS | | 3rd CLASS |
|---|---|---|
| 46'6 | ADULTS | 36'0 |
| 33'0 | CHILDREN | 26'9 |
| | (under 14 years) | |

| TIME TABLE | | | | |
|---|---|---|---|---|
| WATERLOO - | dep. 9.00 a.m. | WINCHESTER - | arr. 2.25 p.m. | |
| SALISBURY - | arr. 10.46 „ | „ | dep. 5.20 „ | |
| „ - | dep. 1.15 p.m. | WATERLOO - | arr. 6.44 „ | |

**FEATURES OF THE TOUR**

Motor Coach Drive in City of Salisbury and to Stonehenge, passing Old
Sarum en route. Visits at Salisbury Cathedral and Stonehenge. Lunch
on train between Salisbury and Winchester. Tour on foot in Winchester City with visits to the Cathedral and College and seeing other
historic buildings, such as the Castle, City Cross, the Westgate, etc.
Tea on train from Winchester to London. Services of guides throughout.

★

As the number of seats available is limited, tickets should be obtained
in advance at Waterloo, Victoria or Charing Cross S.R. Stations, from
Messrs. Thos. Cook & Son, Ltd., Berkeley Street, W.1.
or any Travel Agent.

thus it was probably only being used to 'back up' the manual jacking operations. The wood blocks on the running plate are to stop the running plate from being damaged as the engine was being raised. As with all breakdown recovery teams, they are only too keen to take the 'Hot spanner' to anything that gets in their way......and it may not have been necessary to cut the RHS boiler handrails, but they probably presented an obstruction to the top of the jack when the engine was still leaning over.

"I am surprised at the proximity of the ground staff in the picture on page 76 - to the pulling gear which is clearly under tension. To be fair, the engine is now standing on the bullhead rails and thus the pulling force being deployed will be relatively low compared to just dragging it along the ground. The block and tackle equipment being used is very similar to the Kelbus gear that was originally developed (I think) by a LMS / LMR shedmaster and a driver colleague, who subsequently set up a small business to supply the equipment to the rail industry. Prior to this equipment being introduced 'sheer grunt' in terms of several engines was often deployed – in dragging derailed vehicles back to the 'railway' or at least within the reach of breakdown cranes etc. As with any block and tackle system the applied pulling force can be relatively small, the pulley system being used to multiply the force over a short pulling distance. What is key here is not how much pulling power that you have but how well you can 'anchor' the other end of the block and tackle i.e. the point at which the reaction to the pulling is being taken – and this was a successful feature of the Kelbus gear with its special track anchorages; thus the weight of the traction being used for the pulling also helped provide the anchorage. An unfortunate feature of these operations is that the actual pulling force being applied can only be guessed at, particularly if you have 100 tons of a loco that is doing the pulling ! and failures of the pulling (more appropriately winching) equipment are / were not uncommon. Back to my original point here, the stored energy in the wire ropes of the pulling equipment can be quite considerable and with little prior warning of a failure. A broken steel wire will whip round scything through anything as soft as the human body - but of course this all took place

*Top left -* The 'Devon Belle' observation car at Wimborne, Brian Kohring / Peter Russell.
*Left -* Handbill of a similar excursion working, Ian Shawyer collection. Colin has further added, "There is an interesting snippet in the current (no 273, summer 2014) issue of the Pines Express (Somerset & Dorset Rly Trust), detailing an excursion on 6 September 1956 from Paddington to Weymouth, outwards via the Salisbury & Dorset, Wimborne and Hamworthy Junction (and back via Soton, Andover and the MSWJt): the stock was supposed to have included an ex-Devon Belle observation car. Clearly the photos you have are of the other train, as is, almost certainly, the one I sent you. Still, it seems as though observation cars through Wimborne were, if not exactly ten a penny, more common than we once thought!"

some 20 years before the Health & Safety at Work Act was introduced.

Lastly, I found the short summary on constituent company bias in SW 25 interesting and I would agree with the comments re causation / expectancy My personal preference has always primarily been the LB&SCR. The SE&CR shortfall is indeed unfortunate and hopefully this can be rectified in the future. Whilst I used to write regular articles for a modern industry publication, I'm afraid that I don't feel qualified enough to be able to write on historical matters......

Hopefully you will find my comments of help to you. I trust that you will be able to keep SW publications going, any chance of a piece on either Brighton or Ashford works ?" *(Some interesting points. Eric Youldon has also kindly send a letter of notes which we hope to include shortly. As regards Brighton / Ashford works pieces - any offers....? - Ed.)*

Now to the snapshots of the mystery Devon Belle observation car workings recorded by J L Farmer at Winchester. This from Colin Divall. "They are almost certainly from August 1952, when the Southern Region ran an excursion to Dorchester. Some years ago Glen Woods supplied me with information from the Railway Observer (September 1952, p.256) in response to an internet query I made about a photo of the same car at Wimborne (attached): "Pullman Excursions - A new excursion this year was run on 20 / 8 / 52, leaving Waterloo at 9.45 am and due Wimborne (via Ringwood) at 12.18 pm Proceeding at 1.45 pm the route was via Broadstone-Hamworthy line to Dorchester (2-30). Here passengers were taken on a coach tour via Bovington and Lulworth to Wareham, where they rejoined the train, which meanwhile had worked empty from Weymouth and back for servicing. Return from Wareham was at 5.45 pm, via Bournemouth. 34008 was used on seven Pullmans (27, 171, *Cassandra*, *Rosemary*, 60, 208 and observation car 13), and the train was noted arriving at Wimborne three minutes early." The photo was taken by the late Brian Kohring, and supplied to me by Peter Russell.

Roger Whitehouse supports this with his own notes, "On the days the 'Devon Belle' did not run, the cars were available for luxury excursions. The following are known to have passed through Winchester:
17-8-49 - 9.0 am Waterloo Salisbury Southampton Winchester return 6.44 pm worked by No. 30865.
12-7-50 - Waterloo Salisbury and Winchester.
18-7-51 - Waterloo Salisbury 1044 am / 1.50 pm, Winchester 3.00 pm – 5.25 pm, Waterloo 6.58 pm.
20-8-52 - 9.45 am Waterloo, Wimborne 12.18 pm / 1.45 pm, Dorchester 2.30 pm, after coach tour depart Wareham 5.45 pm via Bournemouth worked by 34008.

Now from Tony Carter, "Small quirks in the timetable never cease to interest me. I remember at least the 1940s when the GWR public TT was the size and shape of our WTT, while the other companies adopted the small but fat book. Does anyone know when the GWR came into line?

The 2-NOL: 2-BIL article reminded me that the Chichester –Portsmouth stopping service which was operated by a 2NOL or 2 BIL but was listed as a 'Rail Motor'. Just a few years behind the times! One of the most amusing entries which I saw in the SR public time table was a passing time for Spa Road (close to London Bridge). I am sure the public must have been completely baffled. This obviously was an entry imported from the WTT which had crept in by mistake."

Hot off the press comes this from George Hobbs on the colour interlude (Shortlands and the Golden Arrow) that appeared in SW27, 1. "Shortlands Station signalling, p36. This picture dates from just before the rearrangement of the tracks from down-down-up-up to down-up-down-up, as shown by the new, but white crossed, 4-aspect colour light signal on the right with the approaching Orpington train on that line. I think that the Beckenham Junction route has already been converted to colour-light operation and that the distant signals for that route are in the location of the old semaphores. At night the display would be red above yellow with both signals on. With the home signal off, the display would be either yellow or green. The blanking plates would ensure that a pure colour light yellow or green signal would show. Definitely an odd but transitional arrangement. The Catford Loop has not been converted to colour-light operation so the distant arm is still in situ for the splitting signals. 2. 'Golden Arrow'. p38. I beg to differ but this is not Petts Wood. Looking closely the second track from the left is not electrified, so I suggest that this is just south of Sevenoaks Station, which was the limit of electrification in those days. The left hand line is a siding for terminating electric trains on the up side. Next is the unelectrified up main line. The two lines to the right are again electrified for terminating electrics on the down side, with a siding branching off on the edge of the picture."

Jane Sullivan has similarly added, "With reference to the picture on p.36 of SW27, you will notice that the blanked green glass is only in the signals for the route towards Beckenham Junction, as they have colour-light distants below them, so when the semaphore was pulled off the colour-light provided the aspect (yellow or green). The signal towards the Catford Loop has a semaphore distant below it, and so its green glass was not blanked out."

Now from Jeremy Clark, "Hi Kevin, may I add a little spice to Alan Blackburn's excellent resume of the Southern's history in SW27, particularly concerning the changeover from semaphore to colour-light signalling out of Waterloo.. In his book 'Nine Elms Engineman', the late-Bert Hooker has been discussing the occasional 'rolling' propensity of the 'Lord Nelsons'. He goes on to say that Bert Knowles told him when he was firing to Sal Payne in the top link, Sal had been on the sick list during the changeover period. The first time Sal travelled on the new down fast line through Clapham Junction Bert [Knowles], who was firing, noticed as they passed West London Junction that Sal had no apparent intention of slowing down. He called out,

"It's forty through Clapham Sal". But his mate took no notice and Bert said they entered the curve nearer 60mph than the regulation 40: the boiler on the Nelson wanted to go straight on but the main frame and wheels dictated otherwise. The engine went into a roll which was not corrected until Earlsfield. Bert added it was the only occasion that he had seen Sal Payne change colour and said he would not like to experience that again.

"I doubt this was an isolated incident and it says quite a lot about the excellent condition of the track as well as the relative stability of the engines. One wonders how things might have turned out had the Nelson been fitted with coil rather than leaf springs?"

Almost at the end and a comment about our deliberately 'off the wall' book, 'GWR SIGNAL BOX CATS - LIVERIES and ALLOCATIONS'. A note from 'Thomas', " I bought this good book off you a while back and have been meaning to send you a picture of the current allocation at Yeovil Pen Mill Signalbox. I was on the rounds yesterday and popped in for a cuppa with his food, still paid for by Network Rail." - Thomas, Chief Rat & Rabbit Controller YPM.

Finally, whilst we are humbled by the positive comments we receive on 'SW' I will admit we usually remove such words. One though we will include with continuing thanks for all your support. From Alan Morris, "Congratulations on your 25th issue. I've enjoyed your series, and think that it is really hitting its stride. For sheer variety of subject matter, nothing else even comes close. Hope you continue, and all power to you and your contributors. Many Thanks, Alan Morris (a loyal reader).

(Just as we were completing this letters section we received a note from Ian Nolan offering us a number of views of Lancing Works taken on an Open Day in the early 1960s. The intention is to use these as a photo feature in SW29.)

The last word from Jeremy Clarke, "Hi Kevin. I've just come upon a bloopah in the caption to the photo on p72 (SW27). It states the line from Ludgate Jct to Factory Jct is ex-LBSCR. It should, of course, be ex-SECR."

*Above* - Southern 4-PAW unit (or should it be a 4-MOG?) at Yeovil complete with tail traffic.

*Left* - Interior of the old signal box at Winchester (City) and which was replaced in 1966.
Cty Brian Corps / Roger Simmonds.

*Opposite top* - Inspection saloon at Brighton.          Aryan Snowsill

*Opposite bottom* - The Southern Region's solitary BR Standard Class 3 2-6-0, No 77014 which ended its days based at Guildford in July 1967.
          Aryan Snowsill

# THE SELSEY TRAMWAY
## Part 1 by Terry Cole
## 'A Glimpse in the early 1920s.'

**Above** - This atmospheric photo shows 0-4-2ST No 3 'Hesperus' leaving Selsey with a mixed train for Chichester. The locomotive was originally built by Neilson and Co to 3ft 6in gauge for the East Cornwall Mineral Railway. When this system became part of the Plymouth, Devonport and South Western Junction Railway and converted to Standard Gauge in 1908, the locomotive was converted as well. It was purchased by Holman Stephens in 1912 for the Selsey Tramway. Modifications were made in 1916 including new (second-hand) trailing wheels and cab and the boiler was raised by 12 in. It was at this time given the name 'Hesperus' and became No 3 in the Selsey fleet. She apparently gave good service for several years, although pictures of her in traffic are very rare. Withdrawn in 1924 she rusticated in the scrap siding at Selsey, becoming increasingly derelict until broken up in 1932. The leading vehicle in the train is a coke wagon, No 211 from Gardner's Anthracite Collieries at Swansea, presumably for the local gas works. This is followed by No. 2, one of the Hundred of Manhood and Selsey Tramway's own box vans. The passenger part of the train follows in the shape of the LCDR coaches purchased in 1921.

**Opposite** - Here is No 4 heading for Selsey with the three LCDR coaches. This 0-6-0ST locomotive was built by Hudswell Clarke in 1902 and originally carried the name 'Wembley'. After a number of owners, it was purchased by the Selsey Tramway company from Thomas Ward of Sheffield in 1919. This picture was taken before it was involved in the fatal derailment in September 1923, as it has the wooden box like cab it acquired on arrival at Selsey and is not carrying nameplates. Following the accident, it was rebuilt with a different cab, courtesy of one of the other Selsey locos and was named 'Chichester' (2nd). However it did little further work and was scrapped in 1932. *Both photographs Terry Cole collection.*

# SELSEY

## Part 2 by Jeffery Grayer

### *Recalling the Shefflex railcars operated on the West Sussex Railway between Chichester and Selsey.*

In mid-January 1935 a sad procession made its way from Selsey to Chichester when 1866 built Manning Wardle 0-6-0ST "Morous" crewed by Driver Harry Davies and Fireman Tom Apps and one of the last two active steam locomotives on the line, hauled the chassis of the Shefflex railcars together with their three plank baggage trailer on their final journey over the increasingly rickety and weed-strewn track of the Hundred of Manhood & Selsey Tramways latterly known as the West Sussex Railway. With their bodies having been previously removed at Selsey, the subsequent fate of which is unknown, the railcar chassis were parked on the headshunt of the transfer siding at Chichester station together with "Ringing Rock" another Manning Wardle tank. The railcars, being the personal property of Colonel Stephens, were not auctioned along with the remainder of the railway's assets in March 1936 but were unceremoniously scrapped. This was all a far cry from 7 years previously when the brand new railcars had arrived on the line in February 1928. The Chichester Observer had reported their arrival when their correspondent advised –

*"For the first time in many months I had the pleasure of travelling down to Selsey once more by the Selsey Tramway – I say it in no spirit of levity – it was a real pleasure. Since "Ebenezer" has been superannuated, she has been replaced by a more up to date vehicle. A Shefflex which has already done much to restore the fair name of the Company for punctuality and well maintains their boast of being the quickest, cheapest and safest route to Selsey."*

They had been ordered by Colonel Stephens in December 1927 from the Shefflex Motor Co. a firm based in Tinsley, Sheffield who primarily produced road vehicles. Shefflex was founded by John Sherwood and the units were constructed at Rutland Street in Sheffield. The bodies were built by W J Flear Ltd of Burton Road, Sheffield at a cost of £158 each. Although originally intended for the Shropshire & Montgomeryshire (S&M) Railway, the units were delivered directly to Chichester, having been loaded onto a pair of flat trucks for the journey from Yorkshire to Sussex, the railway companies of the time having unsurprisingly refused to allow them to move under their own power. Accompanying the railcars was a representative of Shefflex, who took the cars for their initial spin down the line to Selsey and, in doing so, proved that sandboxes were required to assist with braking, the rear wheels having locked on braking, causing the units to slide out of control for some hundreds of yards over a fortunately empty level crossing.

## SELSEY.

**By Road** from Cnichester, 8 miles.

**By Rail.**—A light railway, called the **Hundred of Manhood and Selsey Tramway**, has a terminus a few yards from the main-line station at Chichester. Tickets, are issued on the trains. Between the termini at Chichester and Selsey there are stations at Hunston, Chalder, Sidlesham, Ferry Siding, Selsey Golf Links. This last is only 25 yards from the Club House.

**Golf Links.**—12 holes. (Originally 18. Reduced to 12 in 1917 under the "Cultivation of Lands" Order.) Green Fees: Gentlemen, day, 2s. 6d.; week, 7s. 6d.; month, 20s. Ladies, 1s. 6d., 5s. and 15s. respectively.

*Opposite page - Pictured at Selsey Town station in the early 1930s, the Shefflex railcar set awaits return to Chichester. The locomotive shed can be glimpsed in the left background with Manning Wardle 0-6-0ST "Sidlesham", minus smokebox door, seen protruding from within. (JG)*

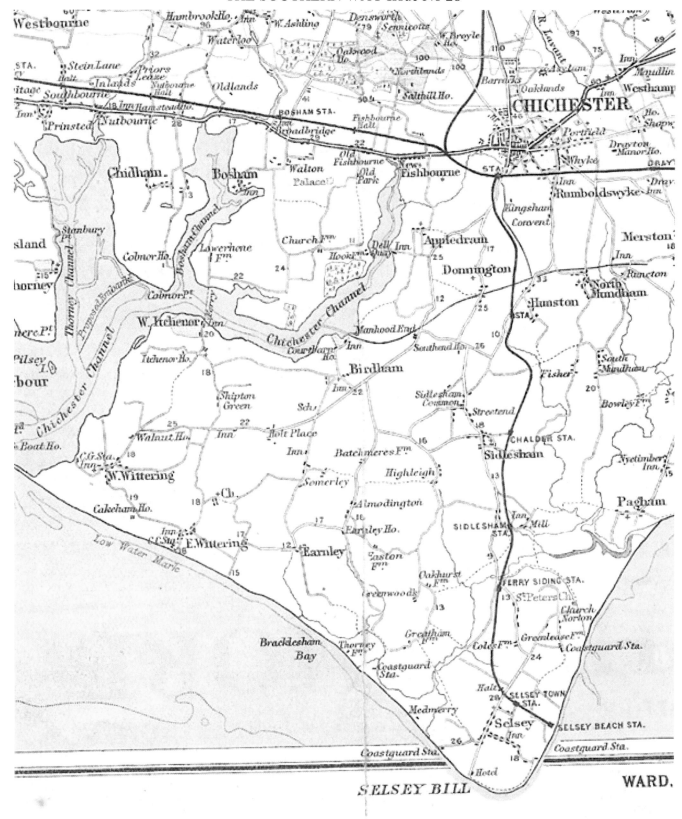

*The route of the WSR which boasted an amazing 10 stations or halts in just 7 miles 61 chains of line. NB Hoe Farm Halt, Mill Pond Halt and Golf Club Halt are not named on the above map.*                    Crown Copyright

*(Worth mentioning is that even the Crown can get it wrong sometimes. On the main line Fishbourne Halt and Bosham Station are mis-placed. Bosham should be about 0.15" eastwards on the E side of the road running N, and Fishbourne Halt should be 0.45" eastwards on the W side of Salthill Road.)*

Railcars were not a new concept to the West Sussex Railway, the first, a Wolseley Siddeley single unit arriving in March 1924 from the Kent & East Sussex Railway, entering service on the 11th of that month. This was soon joined by a Ford motor lorry with which it operated back to back. It was subsequently transferred to the S&M in July 1927. This was followed in 1924 by delivery of a pair of Ford railcars with bodies constructed by Edmunds of Thetford. This experimentation with railbuses pointed the way to the future operation of lightly used rural lines such as that to Selsey, Shefflex cars having first been trialled on the Kent & East Sussex Railway at Rolvenden in 1916. Potentially this form of motive power had its attractions in its markedly lower running costs, when compared with steam, and indeed after a year or so on the line the Shefflex returned a very reasonable running cost of 3.12d per mile covering driver's wages, insurance, repairs etc. in comparison to the 1/4d per mile for steam. As the line's steam fleet fell by the wayside, (of the stock of seven locomotives four had been withdrawn by 1932), the railbuses took over the majority of the workings and by 1934, the final summer of operation, they were handling six of the seven daily departures. They were deemed to be the most effective competition the railway could muster against the more comfortable and convenient Southdown road motor buses.

So what was railcar travel like? An extract from the Railway Magazine of April 1935, although relating specifically to the Ford railcars, may be taken as typical of the passenger experience.

Advertisement from the July 1929 Commercial Motor magazine.

*"The writer had the pleasure (?) of a journey in the Ford car (the Shefflex being under repair at the time) and can vouch for the statement that it was an experience to be remembered. The roar of the engine, the exhaust fumes, the bumping and swaying as the car passed over the uneven track, all combined to impress the journey on the memory. The villagers however, seem inured to it."* Another traveller commented *"It is like being transported in an oil drum leaving one with a continual ringing in the ears, the stench of petrol in the nostrils and an extremely sore behind"*

Inured the villagers may have been but it is apparent from photographs of the railcars in action that those in the know opted for travel in the trailing unit, often separated from the power car by the intervening baggage truck, where they were somewhat insulated from the vibrations, noise and fumes of the driving trailer. The state of the track did not help and passengers often had to hold on to their seats and suffer the trip without talking, as conversation was often rendered impossible by the volume of noise. However, Colonel Stephens always insisted that the railcars were generally reliable and that they "kept to time, giving no nonsense" as well as having the great virtue of being cheap. They also offered the novelty of fine views of the line ahead and astern rather than the sideways

panorama afforded by normal coaching stock. Without the economies realised by the introduction of these railcars, it is questionable whether the railway could have continued for as long as it did. They had the added benfit of reducing average journey times by 5 minutes to a basic 30 minute run between Chichester and Selsey Town.

One of the drawbacks of the railcars was of course the limited passeger capacity with only 23 seats available in each car. This was perhaps not too much of a problem when loadings were declining to a fairly light level, for example a passenger survey undertaken on a couple of Saturdays in 1933 showed that 53 was the highest number of passengers carried on a service from Chichester and 63 on that from Selsey. Resort was had on occasion to use of the intermediate baggage truck to cater for passengers as witness a photograph showing a party of scouts ensconced in the truck on August Bank Holiday 1928. The intermediate truck also carried a variety of goods, including not only passengers' luggage and perambulators, but milk churns, agricultural produce and even a baby calf on one occasion ! It was also used by the permanent way gang as a trolley for track materials.

When delivered the Shefflex cars must have looked very smart painted dark brown with lining out in gold or yellow to the front, rear and side panels together with a white roof. This colour scheme was replaced by one described as red oxide without lining or lettering and by the end they were starting to look a little shabby. Their appearance was not enhanced by the various collisions with motor traffic at the numerous ungated level crossings en route. The pair of headlamps fitted to each car was often missing bulbs or removed completely and the front wooden buffer bar was often photographed with the ends missing or bent as a result of collisions. Gongs were fitted to the offside front bulkheads in 1933 following yet another collision at a road crossing. The 1872 Tramways Act stipulated that trams should be fitted with mechanical bells but the audible means of approach recorded as being fitted to the Shefflex was an exhaust operated whistle. In view of the racket that these units made in motion one would have thought that the unwary road user would have been alerted to the approach of a tram from some distance away ! The company did consider the provision of traffic lights at the ungated crossings but the expense of £39-10s proved too high a price to pay on such an impecunious line for this safety feature.

*Precursor to the railcars was a variety of ancient steam motive power, this example being a Manning Wardle tank of 1861 vintage named "Sidlesham" rebuilt at some stage by Hawthorn Leslie. It is seen here during the somewhat precarious watering procedure undertaken at the Chichester terminus. Water was originally only available from a well at Selsey and from a nearby stream at Hunston but the unreliability of these supplies forced the railway to make use of mains water at Chichester. This locomotive worked services between arrival upon the line in 1907, having been with no less than six previous owners, until scrapped in 1932. Note the unusual upward opening smokebox door necessitated by the height of the bufferbeam in relation to the smokebox opening. She is seen here sporting the wooden casing which the locomotive crew built around the original minimal cab to keep out the worst of the winter weather. This was fitted in 1917 but had been removed by 1923, dating this view to c1921. (H S Brighty. J Grayer Collection)*

*After closure, the Ford railcars were dumped for over a year before their bodies were jacked up onto barrels and the chassis, after being rolled clear, was in all probability cut up on the spot. The bodies were included in the sale catalogue but their subsequent fate is unknown.*

Fares were generally collected by the guard on the railbus this being facilitated by the provision of sliding doors in the rear bulkheads between the two units. The luxury of heating was available to passengers on the line for the first time, provided by hot air pipes warmed by exhaust gases. The majority of the rexine covered seats were of the throw-over type, enabling the queasy passenger to face the direction of travel. Flooring was slatted rather than linoleum covered, as in the Ford units.

Considering they were only 7 years old in 1935 when the end came for the West Sussex Railway one might have expected transfer to the Kent & East Sussex line for further service where railmotors operated until 1938. However, with the K&ESR going into receivership in 1932, railmotor mileage had been slashed and steam hauled mixed trains predominated. Had the preoccupation with economoy not been such a watchword on the Selsey line, could it have survived longer than it did ? The verdict on this must be – unlikely. The Southern Railway was given the opportunity to purchase the concern but declined given what they saw as insurmountable problems. They concluded that if an up to date railcar service, probably using Sentinel units, were introduced, colour light signals installed and repairs to the permanent way effected, then a line speed of 40 mph might be sanctioned with 10 mph applying over the numerous level crossings. There was still considered to be some traffic potential particularly in the summer and on those services connecting at Chichester with London trains which might have been made attractive enough to the commuter. To handle goods it was felt that an SR locomotive could probably be found and diverted over the line to cater for this

traffic. Vital to any resuscitation of the line would be diversion of the track into the main SR station at Chichester to improve connections with mainline trains, a general tidying up of the line to remove the air of dilapidation that prevailed, and the provision of comfortable and attractive rolling stock travelling at a speed competitive with the bus service, the average speed of rail services in the last years of the line being a dismal 14.7 mph. Missing out stops at some of the many intermediate stations, (there were in fact ten in the 7.5 miles between Chichester and Selsey Town) would have speeded up journey times and the SR estimated that theoretically they could do the trip in 23 minutes omitting the halts but calling at all stations. Although the line itself was felt to be unlikely to be self-supporting, the contributory revenue to the SR mainline might just have been enough to tip the balance for, as the report stated, *"The SR cannot expect to share to the full in the developments in Selsey unless there is a rail connection available*." But in the end the SR decided that the risk was not worthwhile, too much needing to be spent on the line with no guarantee that sufficient inroads could be made into the established bus competition to make it a worthwhile proposition. Thus the railway's death warrant was effectively sealed.

Movie footage of the railway is very rare, one snippet being contained on a DVD of "West Sussex Steam" that can be obtained from Chichester Record Office, showing brief glimpses of the Shefflex railcars at Chichester and Selsey. Another brief glimpse, available on YouTube, shows steam locomotive "Morous" and the Ford railcar set.

# Terry Cole's Rolling Stock File No. 28
# Ex LBSCR Coaches on the Isle of Wight

If you have been wondering why LBSCR coaches have featured so little in these files there is a simple answer. Apart from the push-pull sets and electric trains there weren't any on the mainland in the late SR and BR periods. Electrification of much of the 'Brighton' system by the Southern rendered the more modern 'Balloon' stock redundant and it was too big for the rest of the system. Much of the non-corridor stock was antiquated and all LBSCR stock in any event had the non-standard Westinghouse air-brake. So when the opportunity arose it was rebuilt into 'new' electric units, converted to push-pull use or dispatched to the Isle of Wight which did use the air-brake system. The transferred 'Brighton' coaches along with a quantity of SECR stock monopolised the Island's services until the end of steam in 1966.

*Above - This is Composite S6348 seen here at Ryde Esplanade in 1966 now downgraded to a 'second'. It was built in 1924, allocated LBSCR No. 4 but not carried. It entered traffic as SR 6162 and was transferred in 1937 as part of six-coach set 500 for the Ventnor line. It became S6348 to IOW Diagram 373 and was withdrawn in October 1966.*

*Opposite top - One of the five nine-compartment thirds which survived into the 1960s. Built around 1916 it is seen here at Shanklin, by this time the terminus of the Ventnor line, in 1966. Note the long compartment 'grab rails' characteristic of 'Brighton' coaches. One of these vehicles is preserved on the Isle of Wight Steam Railway.*

*Opposite bottom - The LBSCR Brakes came with 4,5,6 or 7 compartments. Here is S 4168 a five-compartment Brake Third at Shanklin in 1966. The body was built in 1922 on a 1905 underframe. It was LBSCR No. 93 then SR number 3870. It was then transferred to the Isle of Wight in 1938 as part of 2-set 502 for the Bembridge branch, IOW Diagram 230. It was withdrawn at the end of steam in January 1967. However it was to be one of the lucky ones and is preserved on the Isle of Wight Steam Railway.* *All photos Terry Cole.*

# Non-Stop: Southampton Central to Wimbledon and then Waterloo

## Richard Simmons

Southern Way No 11 included an excellent article, "Winchester Memories" by Rodney Youngman, together with a plea from our Editor for behind the scenes stories of what went on at such offices as Waterloo, Croydon, Exeter etc. Having worked in the offices at Waterloo and before that at Wimbledon, reminiscences come to hand of life at these former bastions of Southern Region management. Hence the seeds for this article were sown; but insofar as I am concerned it really is a sequel to my series of articles on 'Life in Southampton TSO' to be found in past editions of SW.

In the fourth instalment (SW No 16). I made reference to the district office closure in September 1963 - despite initial management denial - on 30 of that month. As explained in that article, when finishing in the TSO I transferred to the Freight Running (TG) section, where staff were divided to work one Saturday in three. It transpired that I worked on the final Saturday morning, but was cut-off about 10.00 from the outside railway world when a Signal & Telegraph technician arrived unannounced and explained he was "removing the telephone instruments"! So I had to inform the TSO that thereafter they would have to deal with freight matters as they would have done from mid-day in any event.

**We are delighted to continue the story of Richard Simmons and his recollections of working in the Control Office - this time at Wimbledon.**

**The previous instalment (regarding Southampton Control) appeared in 'SW16'.**

### Transfer to Wimbledon

So why, with the London West division office located at Woking, close the two offices and transfer both to Wimbledon? In my opinion this seemed to revolve around yet another concept of management reorganisation, resulting in the birth of Line Managers to replace not only the then District Managers but also part of the headquarters operating and commercial departments at Waterloo. This was relatively simple in the case of the South Eastern and Central divisions. who were simply renamed Line Managers. These two organisations had moved offices from Orpington and Redhill respectively, the South Eastern first to Queen Street close to Cannon Street station and later to Beckenham, the Central to Essex House outside East Croydon station. This last named building was the typical office block which characterised the 1960s and came to dominate the Croydon skyline. Essex House has since been demolished. So, what to do with the Western Section?

This problem would seem to have been partially resolved on 1 January 1963 when all former L&SWR lines west of Salisbury (Wilton South) were transferred and sank into the abyss of Western Region control. Thus the Western Section's western extremity was reduced, from 259 miles from Waterloo to Padstow to 142 miles at Weymouth. With the Exeter Divisional Manager's office no longer in SR territory, and notwithstanding the upheaval to staff involved, no reason existed for Line Managers' organisations at both Woking and Southampton when one would suffice. Thus Wimbledon became the chosen location for the Line Manager's office, although the question might still be asked, why locate it at one end of the area and not somewhere in the middle? I do not know the answer to that question but by going to Wimbledon, it placed all three Line Managers' offices in the London area and close to Waterloo. Perhaps regional management was eager to cut to the minimum travelling time for Line Managers' representatives attending meetings at Waterloo. Today we would probably describe the three office locations as being within the M25: (that giant car park did not exist in those days although by then it may already have started to become a twinkle in road planners' eyes!)

*A few years prior to Richard's time at Wimbledon (and Waterloo) but I could not resist the inclusion of this 1950 view of Taxi's under police direction at Waterloo.*

## Office Layout

The Wimbledon office was located at 19, Worple Road, SW19 in a typical seven storey building of the period, of which only the ground floor was not used exclusively for railway purposes. The majority of the ground floor being occupied by a cash register firm; with at one end entrance to railway-occupied upper floors. Notwithstanding the railway accommodation being floors two to seven, they were numbered one to six. On the first floor was a conference room, finance and work study sections, mail room with small reprographic facilities and staff canteen - of which more later... . The second and third floors housed "commercial" sections such as passenger facilities, parcels and cartage together with staff - thankfully the ghastly term human resources was not in use in the 1960s - and works and modernisation. This latter section dealt principally with station buildings and facilities and at that time seemed to spend much time reducing or even totally removing platform canopies and covers on those footbridges which had them. Accommodated on the fourth floor were operating sections such as passenger and parcels trains, freight (including freight rolling stock), passenger rolling stock, engine diagrams, rules and regulations and electrification & planning. When the Bournemouth electrification was announced this last mentioned section was re-designated simply electrification. At that time guards' rosters still remained domiciled at Waterloo. There was a large typing pool on the fifth floor and the sixth floor housed senior officers.

It goes without saying that over the years some sections were moved around and "squeezed up" especially when the aforementioned Waterloo guards' section was transferred in, and a new train control (as the Train Supervision offices had become) was established on the fourth floor following closure of Woking and Southampton controls. When the control was up and running, we

*More appropriate to the period in question, No 34013 'Okehampton' on the 17.23 Waterloo - Bournemouth running parallel with the 17.30 Waterloo - Bournemouth at the former Bramshot Halt. The latter service is formed of two 4TC units and a 4REP, 17 June 1967.*

*J J McIvor*

ordinary members of staff were prohibited from going in there to see if our homeward trains were likely to run to time!

Victualling - it was Napoleon, I believe, who had once said that an army marches on its stomach: and to a railway worker the equivalent was tea, an important (perhaps vital) ingredient of efficient train working. No doubt etched in the minds of many railway enthusiasts of a certain age will be the memory of footplate crews climbing on to the footplate with, amongst other items in their hand, the all important billy-can of tea. Gallons of tea were consumed in loco-shed bothies, where conditions would have given modern "'elf and safety" inspectors immediate apoplexy. Also not to be forgotten was the egg and bacon fried at the firebox door on a coal shovel. So too, tea was an important commodity in the life of a railway clerk.

When at Southampton there was a communal office gas stove where kettles were boiled but as TSO staff were on shift work a small electric oven of Belling manufacture was provided. Conditions were vastly different at Wimbledon where kettles were forbidden. This was because a catering contractor had been appointed to operate a canteen and provide tea/coffee machines the latter being a relatively new innovation at that time. It was said that kettles were outlawed because the office electrical supply was insufficient to cope with the possibility of numerous such appliances being switched on at the same time. My personal belief was that the catering contractor was thinking more about what effect internally-made tea would have on tea machine profits. Kettles were, nevertheless, covertly smuggled into the office and the tale went round the office that on one occasion, so many kettles were merrily boiling at the same time that fuses were indeed blown on the electrical system. Unsurprisingly this provoked a management crackdown, which in turn produced innovative methods of circumventing the kettle ban.

Part of my time at Wimbledon was in the Special Traffic section, where one such method was practised. A few doors away from the office was a small delicatessen and an agreement was made with the proprietor that he would boil the water. A roster was compiled (the railway must have a roster) whereby a clerk was allocated to convey the kettle, concealed in a shopping bag, to the delicatessen whereupon the proprietor would fill it with water and boil it while the clerk waited. The kettle was then duly carried back to the office and its contents poured into the teapot. In return the Special Traffic section undertook to purchase all ingredients required for tea-making from the delicatessen. If we could help it, we were determined not to have to consume machine-dispensed tea.

As to the canteen itself, I don't think the contractor knew what fresh vegetables were; practically everything served had been frozen at some stage in its journey to the hotplate. I particularly remember the powdered potato reminding me of wartime Pom! So a way had to be found not to use the canteen. Salvation came by way of the next door neighbour being the equivalent office of the then Post Office Telephones, BT - of course - not having been born. This telephone office had a staff canteen which by some way or another a few of our staff had sampled, reporting back how excellent meals were compared with what was on offer in our canteen. So the number of railway people using the Post Office facility gradually grew although, needless to say, it was officially forbidden. A colleague and I did think our number was up as one Christmas approached, for upon entering the canteen one lunch time we were approached by two charming ladies standing at the door who asked us if we had obtained tickets for the forthcoming FREE Christmas lunch. We sensed that to enable the lunch to be free, there was an element of a Post Office subsidy, so we dutifully owned-up that we were railway and not Post Office staff. The ladies informed us that that made no difference as we regularly used the canteen so could have a ticket. Our daily presence in the canteen had obviously been noticed and as I remember, it was an excellent lunch. I relate these events since catering plays, or in those days did play, an important part in office welfare.

## Reorganisations

At this juncture it seems appropriate to explain what seemed to be endless title changes given to District Managers. Their names, locations and telephone numbers were listed in public timetables together with the Docks & Marine Manager and Divisional Marine Managers as well as the hierarchy at Waterloo (General Manager etc). I don't know when this practice commenced but the summer 1939 public timetable lists only "officers" at Waterloo. By the last issued Southern Railway timetable (winter 1947) price 6d, Divisional Superintendents were included. This whole practice was discontinued from the summer 1951 timetable. From the locomotive standpoint, it is interesting to note the Chief Mechanical Engineer (O.V Bulleid) was shown as being at Waterloo, but by 1947 was in fact based at Brighton Locomotive works.

Public timetables referred to in the last paragraph were all prepared at Waterloo but on the last page of Working timetables (WTTs), although prepared at divisional offices, they all bore the name of the Superintendent of Operation at Waterloo. By the summer 1955 issue this had changed to Chief Operating Superintendent and in summer 1959 to Operating Officer.

When Line Traffic Managers (LTMs) were introduced in 1962, WTTs carried the name of the respective LTM and not the Operating Officer. South Western Division WTTs however, differed in the title because in that year WTTs, were still produced at Woking and Southampton and the Southampton passenger timetable referred to the Line Traffic Manager at Waterloo as the transfer to Wimbledon had still to be effected. Meanwhile the freight WTT referred to the Line Manager (not Line Traffic Manager) at Waterloo. By 1963, the last year separate Woking and Southampton timetables were produced, the Line Manager had moved from Waterloo to the new Wimbledon accommodation and both WTTs recognised this.

1964 was therefore the first year one passenger and one freight WTT were produced for the whole SWD under the Line Manager Wimbledon's title. By 1965 Line Managers had become Divisional Managers and WTTs acknowledged this but the Isle of Wight WTT for that year ,although produced at Wimbledon, stuck to the title Line Manager, thus continuing independence from the mainland. I think it needs explaining that, when referring to the year a WTT was introduced, was the date of that year's summer timetable and not 1 January.

By 1966 it was time for the next reorganisation (!) and by then the wheel had turned full circle for a Central Timings Office had been created back at Waterloo who would publish all WTTs. Perhaps headquarters considered these upstart Line Managers couldn't be trusted. This organisation was under the umbrella of the Movements Manager - as the Operating Officer had become - and indeed, the 1966 freight WTT was produced under this banner. So the 1966 passenger WTT was the last (but not quite) to come from Wimbledon and from 1967 all were back at Waterloo. So this devolution did not last for long. Thus the first Bournemouth electrification timetable was completed at Waterloo, although planning started at Wimbledon: but Wimbledon Divisional Manager's office had a last laugh or swan song. This came in the form of a Passenger Train Alterations WTT applicable from 12 June 1967 until 9 July 1967, necessary because of the six week postponement of the introduction of full Bournemouth electrification. I'm sure readers will recall this came about following late completion of the full complement of new and converted rolling stock. This publication contained alterations for Mondays-Fridays and Sundays and complete re-issue of the main line service for summer Saturdays during the period. All this must be railway politics at its best. Complicated to understand? Yes. I agree.

Of course there had to be an exception to all these shenanigans and this came in the form of special traffic notice publications issued by Line Managers/Divisional Managers or whatever title was the order of the day. Such notices came in two forms; printed notices produced by a printer which by necessity had to be prepared about a couple of weeks in advance and despatched to the printer. These were issued once weekly, numbered consecutively from 1 at the beginning of a year and adding the year of issue. Additional notices were issued to cover bank holiday periods, special events and major engineering works. These were generally referred to as P notices.

The second publication was issued daily and in those days typed on stencils by the office typing pool. These too were numbered consecutively from 1 at the beginning of the year and prefixed SN being generally known as stencil notices. Such notices were necessary to publicise short notice alterations. It is easy to imagine there was an elaborate system of despatch for these notices to ensure they reached those stations and signal boxes etc requiring them. Until the end of 1962 P notices had the Superintendent of Operation's name on the front page.

The other notice to mention was produced by the Rules and Regulations section and referred to as the P/EW notice and numbered on the same basis as the special traffic P notice but in its own series. It contained details of temporary speed restrictions and sections of lines closed for engineering work, together with minor alterations for signalling and abolition of points and sidings etc. With the demise of Divisional Managers in the 1980s all such publications were centred on regional headquarters at Waterloo and were published under the Chief Operating Manager/Regional Operating Manager's title. So ends the saga of printed notices and one wonders if they are produced today but no doubt all such information is now disseminated by electronic means.

Waterloo HQ produced all engine and carriage "permanent" workings and as has been explained, Divisional Managers produced WTTs, special traffic notices and associated carriage workings for their respective districts: but engine workings remained at RHQ level. For instance, Southampton district office produced special traffic notices for banana train programmes but details had to be telephoned to RHQ who compiled engine workings. When Line Managers came into being, they embraced all this work but to do it, staff were required from RHQ and DM's level necessitating staff transfers. Management mounted a concerted campaign to persuade district office staff to transfer to their respective Line Manager's office but as far as Southampton office staff were concerned there were relatively few takers. The principal objection being the higher cost of housing in the London area compared with "out in the sticks", although a handful did move house to such areas where I live (Farnborough), which are just outside the immediate London area, and an even lesser number (such as myself, initially) went into "digs" in such areas as Wimbledon and Croydon. Nevertheless about half a dozen intrepid members of staff elected to travel daily from the Southampton/Eastleigh area, not the easiest of journeys when Bournemouth electrification work was gathering momentum. For this was the era of declining standards of steam engine maintenance and extended journey times once electrification had been announced. For these people the morning journey was an arduous one, starting on the 06.30 Totton-Winchester City (as Winchester station was then known) DEMU, which with the 1963/64 winter timetable, was extended to Basingstoke principally, it has to be said, for staff purposes. At Basingstoke a change was necessary into the steam-hauled 07.30 Basingstoke-Waterloo and during winter months several accounts were given of freezing conditions on this train, when the steam heating wasn't functioning as efficiently as it should or even functioning at all. As this train was non-stop Woking to Waterloo a further change was necessary into the 07.48

*No 73065 joining the main line at Wimbledon with milk tanks from Morden, 29 May 1963.*

Haslemere-Waterloo but this was not the end of changing, yet another one being necessary at Surbiton to reach Wimbledon courtesy of a Hampton Court -Waterloo service, although some may have continued on the Basingstoke train to Waterloo from where they returned to Wimbledon. Hence you see what I mean by describing this journey as arduous.

For the homeward journey, three days a week ex-Southampton people were permitted to leave the office in time for the down "Royal Wessex" which departed Waterloo at 16.35. The remaining two working days were long ones, as to balance working hours, Southampton people had to remain at their desks and travel home on the 18.30 ex-Waterloo.

Whilst ex-Woking staff had easier journeys, it goes without saying that it took longer to get to and from Wimbledon. To ease their homeward journey, however, the "shoulder peak" 16.47 Waterloo-Alton was revised to start at 16.44 and make an additional stop at Wimbledon - it normally ran non-stop Waterloo to Walton-on-Thames - thus enabling staff to reach Woking and connect with main line services. Perhaps this was part of the negotiating

process to entice staff to move to Wimbledon, but I cannot help thinking that if a passenger had requested such an additional stop the request would have been declined.

Bournemouth electrification vastly improved travelling times for Wimbledon staff but there was one additional out-of-course stop. Waterloo-Bournemouth stopping trains were normally non-stop between Waterloo and Surbiton, but the 16.42 ex-Waterloo called at Wimbledon, so not surprisingly became dubbed "the staff train". As this stop was not part of the normal stopping pattern of these trains, I suppose it was inevitable that the odd occasion arose when the stop was overlooked by the driver and we staff could do no more than watch the train thunder through Wimbledon. One or two more additional stops were made at Wimbledon when the TSOs (by then Controls) transferred to Wimbledon for staff signing on or off duty during the early morning and late evening.

District Manager's offices met their demise on 30 September 1963 but I still have a copy of the final Southampton-issued stencil special traffic notices issued on the preceding Friday 27 September. They contained

111

*At the opposite (Eastern) end of the complex, No 77014 on engineer's duties at Durnsford Road, 19 March 1967.*

*R E Ruffell*

alterations to engineering works that weekend, parcels trains alterations, freight train alterations, party traffic reservations, cover for the Southampton Central Area Manager's annual leave arrangements and the following interesting light engine movements all on 28 September: Nos. 76031 and (U) 31618 Guildford to Eastleigh via Woking, No. 33031 (Ql) Three Bridges to Eastleigh via Havant, No. 41320 Eastleigh to Brighton and No. 33038 (Ql) hauling No. 30518 (H16) from Feltham to Eastleigh.

There was also a rolling stock notice. It seems most likely that the engines going to Eastleigh were destined for withdrawal. In retrospect it seems a pity that no mention was made on these notices that they were the last to be produced by the Southampton office but perhaps officialdom prohibited it. Wimbledon produced their own from the following Monday.

**TO BE CONTINUED...**